Praise for

PURPOSE MEETS EXECUTION

and LOUIS EFRON

"Even in today's hypercompetitive business environment, extraordinary companies aren't satisfied solely with making a profit. These trailblazing companies tap into the unifying influence of purpose to outperform and out maneuver their competition. If you're at all interested in catapulting your company to greater heights and inspiring your employees, listen to and act on what Efron has to say about the unifying powers of purpose."

—Shawn Murphy, Author of *The Optimistic Workplace*;
Founder and CEO, Switch+Shift

"In an era where 'purpose-driven' has become one of the hottest corporate buzz phrases, ***Purpose Meets Execution*** provides a valuable service to business leaders: connecting the dots between organizational purpose and operations. The market is flooded with books about purpose, but few of them unlock the difficult challenge of operationalizing purpose by architecting it into your company's systems and processes. Through copious examples and helpful tools, ***Purpose Meets Execution*** helps unravel the mystery behind the financially successful purpose-driven organization."

—Eric Severson, Former Co-CHRO and Senior Vice President,
HR Gap Inc.; U.S. Department of Commerce Appointee,
United States Department of Commerce; National Advisory
Council on Innovation and Entrepreneurship

"Louis Efron's ***Purpose Meets Execution*** is an enjoyable book that will inspire the reader to be strategic and intentional when focusing on purpose to drive results. The action items are both digestible and easily executable, and follow from real-world examples that illustrate the importance of a shared purpose in a high-performance work culture. The questions posed at the end of each chapter require introspection, and alone are worth the price of the book!"

—Matthew Fehling, President and CEO,
Better Business Bureau

"***Purpose Meets Execution*** provides a refreshing perspective on the topic of business strategy and leadership. Efron does a great job in showcasing a blueprint with which an organization can build a foundation to support high growth, sustainability, and humanity. Stressing the power of influence that leaders have over their company's culture and work environment, the book provides a toolbox of techniques and tools that will drive positive social and economic change as well as business results."

—Dr. Emad Rahim, Kotouc Family Endowed Chair and
Associate Professor, Bellevue University; Fulbright Scholar

"Read ***Purpose Meets Execution***, follow its wisdom, and make your competition irrelevant! Louis Efron's vast experience and insights (gained across industries) are synthesized into a resource that will help you turn your leadership vision into reality. ***Purpose Meets Execution*** offers practical tools and insights for strategic planning, disciplined operations, practical innovation, and sustainable success. What are you waiting for? Isn't it time to inspire purpose and hardwire operational excellence?"

—Joseph Michelli, Ph.D. CCXP, *New York Times* #1 best-selling
author of *Driven to Delight*, *The Starbucks Experience*,
and *The New Gold Standard*

"What a wonderful book! We all start off with purpose in our businesses and work, a passion for what we do, but that isn't enough. We need to be able to execute on that passion. In ***Purpose Meets Execution*** Louis Efron lays out a clear roadmap for success. It will make you think and it will help you to succeed."

—Chester Elton, *New York Times* best-selling author of *The Carrot Principle*, *All In*, and *What Motivates Me*

"Efron nailed it! ***Purpose Meets Execution*** is a game changer for every organization, today and in the future. It is relevant, inspiring, and actionable. You won't find a book that better captures the elements and actions needed for a highly successful and sustainable organizational culture and business. A must read!"

—Melissa Daimler, SVP, Talent Acquisition and Development, WeWork

"Rarely does a book capture why company culture matters like ***Purpose Meets Execution***. Efron not only makes a profound case for how you need to know why you are in business, but also gives crucial, actionable steps that will certainly lead any organization toward thriving well into the future. Those who read this will find more than stories of how others have prospered in business through having a culture of purpose. They will discover how they can begin to write their own story that will impact their own business and the world they have a heart to serve."

—Ryan McCarty, Cofounder, Culture of Good

"***Purpose Meets Execution: How Winning Organizations Accelerate Engagement and Drive Profits*** is a great balance of reflective thought and the need to move business forward through action. Louis does an amazing job getting leaders to answer the tough questions for themselves and their business. Given the agility required in today's environment, it's critically important for leaders to take the time to find alignment; this book helps them do just that."

—Lacey Leone McLaughlin, Director, Center for Effective Organizations at the Marshall School of Business, USC

"Execution on its own isn't enough. And Core Purpose (your 'why') in the absence of 'how' isn't enough either. Louis shares an important perspective, showing us how to engage both the heart—purpose—and the mind—execution—and how to keep them in balance to drive both culture and growth."

—Cameron Herold, Author of *Double Double*, *Meetings Suck*, and *The Miracle Morning for Entrepreneurs*

PURPOSE
MEETS
EXECUTION

PURPOSE MEETS EXECUTION

How Winning Organizations Accelerate Engagement and Drive Profits

LOUIS EFRON

First edition published in 2017
by Bibliomotion, Inc.
711 Third Avenue New York, NY 10017, USA
2 Park Square, Milton Park, Abingdon, Oxon OX14 4RN, UK

Routledge is an imprint of Taylor & Francis Group, an informa business

Printed on acid-free paper

International Standard Book Number-13: 978-1-138-04909-3 (Hardback)

Library of Congress Cataloging-in-Publication Data
A catalog record for this book has been requested

Visit the Taylor & Francis Web site at www.taylorandfrancis.com
and the CRC Press Web site at www.crcpress.com

Printed and bound in the United States of America by Sheridan

For my mother and father, who put me on this planet, and my wife, Evie, and daughters, Anya Rose and Ella Brae, who make being here meaningful, fun, and magical.

Contents

Foreword

Based on my work with JetBlue, Southwest Airlines, Disney, and other top companies, I know what winning organizations and cultures look like. This is why I was excited when Louis Efron asked me to write this foreword for his book. *Purpose Meets Execution: How Winning Organizations Accelerate Engagement and Drive Profits* perfectly captures the culture and mindset required for all winning and successful organizations now and in the future. Efron's insightful, fresh perspective takes the organizational purpose movement to the next level—combining purpose with executional excellence to fulfill it.

There are many thought leaders speaking about the transformational qualities of organizational purpose and why it is important, but few can tell you what to do next or how to run a business to fulfill it. Efron can and does. His experience as a global human resources executive and business leader in multiple industries—big and small—as well as his published thought leadership, gives him a unique and qualified perspective. It also gives him access to some of the most celebrated brands in business. Efron's stories from Gap, Starbucks, KPMG, Deloitte, O.C. Tanner, National Life Group, Ceridian, Clif Bar, Big Ass Solutions, Johnny Cupcakes, and others bring his concepts to life in a colorful and entertaining way.

Efron walks his readers through simple and easy-to-follow steps, from defining an organizational purpose to fulfilling it through executional excellence—accelerating people engagement and driving profits. He also includes helpful tools along the way, like his six unique interview questions to help hiring managers make better, purpose-aligned hires and chapter questions to highlight areas of opportunity within any business. Organizations of all sizes will benefit and thrive by implementing the ideas and steps found between the covers of this book.

There is more to business than making money, but organizations can't survive without it. Companies must make money to fulfill their purpose, but a business focused solely on financial metrics will struggle to achieve them. In most cases, such organizations swap short-term gain for long-term sustainability, as Efron points out. Those businesses that focus on superb execution in line with their organization's purpose create sustainable, impressive results.

Winning organizations now and in the future understand that investing in making the world a better place, not just stuffing organizational coffers with cash, will produce even greater results and business success. Customers want to buy from such organizations, and the best talent is attracted there, too.

As Efron says, "To truly change the world, you must run a great business." This could not be truer. Money fuels capitalism, but if invested correctly, it also brings about positive social and economic change. In the turbulent world we live in today, we need this idea more than ever. An attitude of profits without purpose is harmful to humanity. It is also unsustainable. Organizations must have a balance of both. This is where Efron's powerful and transformational model comes into play.

Purpose Meets Execution: How Winning Organizations Accelerate Engagement and Drive Profits creates an opportunity for all organizations and business leaders around the globe to up their game by accelerating people engagement and driving profits. It gives companies a way to align their talent attraction and retention, people development, and business strategy with meaningful outcomes for customers and communities, as well as for those working for the organization. Most importantly, it allows businesses a way to measure and improve their balance between a focus on why they are in business in the first place—their purpose—and getting the right things done to fulfill that purpose.

If you want to create a winning organization with sustainable results, you need to read and implement the ideas and steps in this important and timely book.

Ann Rhoades
Cofounder of JetBlue, president of People Ink,
and author of *Built on Values*

Introduction

If you want something new, you have to stop doing something old.
—Peter Drucker

Business today is up against a myriad of complexities: disruptive competition and technologies, volatile economic forces, and a complex and evolving workforce. There is unending pressure to do more with less and deliver short-term goals while driving long-term sustainability, all the while finding and retaining top talent to get it done. Learning how to navigate these pressures is the difference between a thriving business and a dying one. To break out, businesses need to rethink their fundamental drivers for success. In today's world, the most powerful driver of success is a culture of purpose combined with executional excellence.

Based on more than two decades of work, study, and research in the areas of people engagement and strategic human resources, plus extensive experience in the rapidly evolving purpose movement, I have determined the following: organizations with a strong sense of purpose but an inability to execute will ultimately die. Organizations that are expert executors but fail to understand and see the value of purpose will never reach their full potential.

Both purpose and execution are foundational when it comes to highly successful and sustainable organizations. Purpose is simple: it's why an organization was started in the first place—why it exists.

Every organization starts with a purpose, but many lose track of it along the way. In the hustle and bustle of operations, it's easy to forget to focus on the bigger picture. Execution is tricky, too: it's the actions that must occur to fulfill an organization's purpose, occurring in the right pattern and accomplished by the right people. Execution is ultimately measured by an organization's ability to get the right things done.

During my career working in retail, food services, the arts, eleven years at the Fortune 300 medical device company Stryker, the software industry, and most recently at Tesla Motors, I have seen a lot. I experienced and learned a lot. I oversaw every function of a business as a human resources leader, led all human resources capabilities, and ran my own businesses. I spent a significant amount of time serving and entertaining others, selling and watching others sell, and shadowing employees in manufacturing teams and surgical operating rooms. Plus, I travelled and lived around the world. My journeys taught me a lot about the importance of both purpose and execution in organizations and industries around the globe.

When I think of teams that must balance purpose and execution effectively, the most powerful example that comes to mind is from my time in the medical industry. In a hospital trauma ward, there is one clear purpose: save lives. There is no debate over this. Everyone in the operating room works together to achieve the goal. Silos, office politics, and out-of-control egos are dangerous and need to be set aside. The team innately understands that they should never fail to save a life simply from a lack of coordinated effort or a failure to act. And because their purpose is central to the mission, they know that every action needs a connection to fulfilling the shared purpose of saving a life.

That's why superb execution is essential. Purpose alone will not get the job done. Like a heart without a brain, purpose without the ability to accomplish the right things is useless. A brain without a heart dies. Without heart, execution lacks empathy and care. Both the heart—purpose—and the mind—execution—need to work in balance to save a life. It's a principle that applies to the surgeon's table, the boardroom, and your office stand-up—and everywhere in between.

The importance of the heart and mind balance is part of nature's DNA, too. Bees have a clear purpose to pollinate flowers, vegetables, fruits, and nuts. In North America, at least 30 percent of the food consumed depends on bees' abilities to fulfill their purpose. Their purpose is also essential to the production of meat and dairy, as they pollinate the alfalfa and clover crops that feed cattle. Their effective execution—intent, coordination, and ability that ultimately fulfill their purpose—is estimated to be worth around $16 billion in the United States alone. Just imagine what the world would be like without bees—or with bees that lack either purpose or execution.

This same principle applies to all living things, including organizations. If organizations with a strong identified purpose can't execute to fulfill it, they will die. If organizations that have mastered the art of execution lose sight of the reason they started in the first place, they will never realize their true potential.

All organizations and industries have a purpose. Effective execution can be learned and engineered. The most challenging part has proven to be the simple focus on these two tenets in tandem. Some organizations and leaders have yet to buy in to the purpose-based organizational model. As you will learn in this book, those leaders and organizations—no matter how well-established or affluent—are at risk of extinction in the evolving economy. The organizations intent on trying to change the world without an ability to execute will suffer the same fate.

Balancing purpose and execution in an organization is critical not only to its business success and sustainability but to the fulfillment of people working for the business, customers, and societal expectations. Igniting this fulfillment accelerates people and customer engagement and drives profits. Profits allow organizations to reinvest in their business, hire more like-minded people, sell more products or services, and ultimately grow, fulfill their purpose, and win.

Jeremy Blank is a partner and national talent leader in the Tax Services Group at Deloitte, the world's largest professional services firm, which employs seventy thousand professionals in the United States with audit, financial advisory, tax, and consulting services. He shares:

> At Deloitte, we're keenly aware of our professional services purpose, but we're also committed to the purposeful execution of our business strategy. Deloitte's strategy addresses our clients, stakeholders, and communities. It balances a corporate vision and purpose with how we deliver value—that is to say, how we get the job done.
>
> It's important that organizations define their purpose, as well as how they apply this purpose to client service. A balance between organizational purpose and business execution is critical to this equation. Organizations may be required to make tough decisions that are challenging in the short-term, but are better aligned with their long-term purpose.
>
> An important part of Deloitte's succession planning is our "NextGen" leadership development program. "NextGen" is a group of roughly fifty high-potential partners and principals nominated each year by function CEOs. NextGen develops leaders who are sensitive to decisions that align both with purpose and execution. Deloitte's "NextGen" program ensures its future leaders understand the importance and unwavering commitment of client service, talent development, and citizenship, and that true organizational success is predicated on success in each of these three areas. Our most successful leaders are not only sensitive to our purpose, but they're also able to maintain the balance between the purpose and its execution.

In this book, you will find a simple framework that merges the power of a purpose-driven organization with executional excellence. By applying what you learn, you will be able to determine whether your company has a clear and meaningful sense of organizational purpose and whether that purpose is effectively aligned with business practices across functional areas. You will then be able to use the model presented to address gaps and create a plan to bring more balance to your organization, accelerate people and customer engagement, and drive profits.

When companies understand and implement a plan and process to balance purpose and execution, they create an unbeatable competitive advantage in the market. They pave the way to finding and retaining the best of the current and next-generation workforce, delight customers, and deliver exceptional and sustainable results.

The ability to balance purpose and execution in every organization and industry—for-profit and not-for-profit, big or small, established or start-up—has proven to be the single most powerful factor that delivers success and sustainability to organizations and industries of all kinds around the globe.

Throughout this book I refer to "people" rather than "employees" wherever possible. I do this for a very specific reason. Technology and the workforce mindset are rapidly evolving. Workers around the globe are asking for new and dynamic definitions of work, and companies are answering—in positive and evolving ways. This dynamic will make the traditional "employee"—a nine-to-five, sitting-in-a-cubicle, business-casual-clad person—a much smaller segment of the future workforce.

Even now, we can see the work evolution beginning. From a technology standpoint, people already are embracing remote work. In the not-so-distant future, they will sit around a conference table virtually with others who are physically spread across the globe. Soon, people will be able to regularly print physical objects from their home printer instead of frequenting the corner store. Or project engineers will walk around or even experience large physical spaces or objects from thousands of miles away. This will not only be a lifestyle benefit, it will create massive organizational cost savings and increased profits.

Ray Kurzweil, Google's director of engineering and a noted futurist, claims that by the 2030s we will be able to link and upload our brains to cloud computers.[1] At that point, commuting daily to an office space somewhere will seem absurd. Whether or not you agree with his thinking, workplace trends are ever changing and are moving in the direction of less traditional offices, employees, and management structures. Already, certain companies exist entirely online—with networks of remote people who keep in contact via the web. Imagine what the next few decades can bring.

Remote working is no surprise, either, to anyone who understands the psychology of current workers. As technology encroaches on personal time, the line between work and home life is more and more blurred—and individuals want the ability to control that boundary no matter the time of day or the location they work from. Mindsets are shifting, too. The next-generation workforce wants more freedom and flexibility in life.[2] In fact, studies show that as many as 72 percent of millennials want to be their own boss.

The crossroads between these two evolutionary forces will spur new workplace relationships. The traditional "employee–employer" association will transform into more contractor or vendor partnerships. The "employee" may even become a thing of the past. However, people will always be part of the equation. That is why people are the focus of this book—because, regardless of their official capacities, they're the ones who innovate, encourage, question, and create.

At the end of each chapter you will find a "Chapter Questions" section. This section is intended to provide tools you can immediately use and questions to think about in your business. Their purpose is to guide you through your journey to understanding what purpose and execution look like in your organization and how you can bring both into balance to achieve accelerated and lasting results.

Take time to ask, think on, answer, and apply these questions. I recommend thinking about and sleeping on your answers to any questions for a day or two. Plus, share your thoughts with your colleagues, team, friends, and family. The insights you gain from others close to you will prove to be invaluable. Most importantly, enjoy your journey. That is where the true magic happens.

Notes

1. Solomon Israel. "Artificial Intelligence, Human Brain to Merge in 2030s, Says Futurist Kurzweil." *CBC News*, June 5, 2015. www.cbc.ca/news/technology/artificial-intelligence-human-brain-to-merge-in-2030s-says-futurist-kurzweil-1.3100124.
2. Rob Asghar. "What Millennials Want in the Workplace (And Why You Should Start Giving It to Them)." *Forbes*, January 13, 2014. www.forbes.com/sites/robasghar/2014/01/13/what-millennials-want-in-the-workplace-and-why-you-should-start-giving-it-to-them/#130bb0352fdf.

PART I

Building an Unshakable Foundation

CHAPTER 1

Starting with Purpose

All great organizations are built on a meaningful purpose.

—Louis Efron

Everything starts with a purpose—in your personal life and in business. As a foundational idea, purpose has strong roots in religion, is a buzzword in personal development, and is becoming the dominant theme in business today. Despite this, few people have read a definition of the word. Let's begin by reviewing and understanding its specific meaning as a baseline to the platform of Purpose Meets Execution.

There are three clear definitions of purpose I like to use:

- The *Merriam-Webster Dictionary* definition: "The reason for which something is done or used: the aim or intention of something."[1]
- Aristotle's definition: "Where your talents and the needs of the world cross."[2]
- The accepted definition in the purpose movement: "The reason your organization/industry exists. Your *why*."

The first definition generally defines purpose. The second one applies to you, an individual, specifically: how you will change the world by being the person you were intended to be—fulfilling your personal purpose. The third definition addresses how an organization is trying to change the world—why it started in the first place.

The way the last two definitions work together is key to accelerating people engagement in your organization. Imagine if every person from your receptionist to your CEO jumped out of bed each morning excited to start work. They couldn't wait to tackle the day because they believed they were fulfilling their personal purpose, a purpose aligned with the job and organization they work in. Imagine the power that would create for your organization, your community, and the economy as a whole.

Take the following story as an example.[3]

In the 1960s, President John F. Kennedy was touring the NASA space center. As he was walking the facility, he saw a janitor highly engaged in sweeping the floor. JFK approached the man and asked him what he did at NASA. The janitor stopped what he was doing, looked Kennedy in the eyes, and said, "Well, Mr. President. I'm helping put a man on the moon."

How great would it be if every person in your business felt like this janitor? How would productivity improve? Work quality? Commitment? Retention? Sales? Profits? Thirty years of research say that kind of inspired commitment would have a significant positive impact on your organization's business results.

People like NASA's janitor are not complaining about their company or job. They are not asking for more money if they are being paid a fair wage. They are spending their time trying to figure out how to do better work, add more value, and help fulfill their organization's purpose. In fact, in Daniel Pink's book *Drive*, he concludes that as long as people feel they are being compensated adequately and fairly, compensation is a low factor in engagement.[4] More important to people motivation—in all areas of our lives—is the human need "to direct our own lives, to learn and create new things, and to do better by ourselves and our world," Pink says.

In his book, Pink highlighted a 1969 study by Edward Deci, then a Carnegie Mellon University psychology graduate student, that determined, "When money is used as an external reward for some activity, the subjects lose intrinsic interest for the activity." The controversial study incentivized students with money to solve puzzles. Those who were paid for their work showed less interest in the activity and spent less time trying to complete the task. Pink asserts that the traditional carrot-and-stick management approach of external rewards like money can be damaging to people engagement in several ways, including: extinguishing intrinsic motivation, diminishing performance, crushing creativity, crowding out good behavior, encouraging cheating or unethical behavior, becoming addictive, or fostering short-term thinking. In all cases, personal meaning trumps external drivers when it comes to people engagement and performance.

The ROI of Purpose

There are still skeptics when it comes to living a purpose-driven life or leading a purpose-focused business. Some think it is a soft and fluffy concept—one perhaps reserved for religious zealots. However, in business, as in life, the ROI has proven strong. On the organizational front, research studies in the book *Firms of Endearment*, by Rajendra Sisodia, David B. Wolfe, and Jagdish N. Sheth, determined the following:

- Corporate purpose is the single most powerful tool for growing an organization's top and bottom lines.
- Purpose-driven companies grew their businesses 1,681 percent between 1998 and 2013 compared with the Standard and Poor's 500, which averaged 118 percent during that period.

Some of the most recognized brands, including Ikea, Costco, IDEO, Whole Foods, and Commerce Bank, were included in the study. The results were matched only by a similar study a few years earlier. In every case, organizations that chose to focus on purpose over profits achieved accelerated business results—proving that purpose truly matters to an organization's growth, success, and sustainability.

A 2013 Deloitte study titled *Culture of Purpose: A Business Imperative* makes this point: "What companies do for clients, people, communities, and society are all interconnected. A culture of purpose ensures that management and employees alike see each as a reason to go to work every day."[5]

Deloitte's study also concludes that companies that have a strong sense of purpose as perceived by their employees also have a history of strong financial performance, high employee engagement, and satisfied customers. In companies where employees said their organization lacked a strong sense of purpose, financial performance, employee engagement, and customer satisfaction were significantly lower.

More Than a Buggy Whip

An organizational purpose is timeless. Products and strategies may change, but a purpose does not. I was once asked about the purpose of a buggy whip company from time gone by. Was it not to produce the best buggy whips in the world? My response was a resounding, "No!"

From my perspective, the purpose of a buggy whip company was to get a customer from point A to point B—from home to work and back again, to a holiday in the country, to visit a friend or relative, or to deliver goods to customers. Wherever someone may want to go, a buggy whip company would provide a tool—in the original case, a horsewhip—to help people arrive at their destinations. The purpose—and its focus—is timeless. It transcends buggies and would be preserved when electric cars first appeared on the roads in the late 1800s, when mass market gasoline vehicles arrived soon after, and when electric cars came back in the 2000s—and it would continue when fully autonomous hover crafts appear in 2050 and teleporting devices in 2075. The products and strategies may change, but the purpose remains constant—to get someone to a destination. Unfortunately, most buggy whip companies did not embrace such an overreaching purpose and died with the advent of automobiles.

A good organizational purpose statement captures the reason your business was started in the first place in a succinct, timeless, and undeniable way. For example, the auto industry's purpose is "to keep the world moving." Like the buggy whip company example, this purpose covers all forms of transportation that may ever be dreamt up. The banking industry's purpose is "to improve life for people, families, organizations, and communities through financial services." Again, this purpose would encompass an economy backed by gold bars or bitcoins. Its purpose is timeless, and the pursuit of fulfilling it continues from generation to generation. It is sustainable.

If the purpose of your organization has a shelf life or specific period of time connected to it, you most likely have it wrong. Start thinking more broadly. Connect your idea to a higher plane. If you are going to invest the time, money, and energy to start a business or industry, you want it to survive you and grow well into the future. A business should never fail because it is trying to fulfill the wrong purpose. If it does, it is fundamentally broken to begin with. A strong and undeniable purpose should be core to your organization's DNA—the foundation from day one. This is the foundation your execution will build upon.

People working for your company and customers should know and understand how your organization contributes to the world and believe its existence is necessary.

Walmart is a great example. Twenty-four hours a day, the company goes about its business "to save people money so they can live better."[6] Everything it does supports that purpose.

The company's corporate office is functional but lacking in costly bells or whistles. All the employees, including executives, empty their own trash bins. Stores resemble warehouses with just what is needed to hold products for sale. Fancy trimmings or extra amenities are simply not part of Walmart's formula.

Because Walmart's purpose and supporting culture is clear and undeniable, both customers and job candidates know exactly what to expect coming in the door. This expectation helps drive the right customers and people to the organization. If you like high-end retail shopping, you won't go to Walmart. If you like working in a posh environment and having someone else empty your trash, you won't apply to Walmart. If you are not passionate about saving money, Walmart won't be the best fit for you, and your success at the company will be limited.

Creating proper alignment with employees starts with Walmart's recruiting. If people come in the door and are personally cost-conscious and frugal, they will remain that way through their careers at the company. If they truly care about saving money, they will work hard to ensure it happens at the organization and for its customers. They will believe what the organization believes. This will translate into an honest and personal connection with Walmart's purpose and a sincere interest in helping fulfill it. Fulfilling the retail giant's purpose means selling more products to more people, becoming more profitable, and continuing the cycle.

To achieve the clarity of purpose that Walmart has, your organization's purpose communication should do three things:

1. Provide a clear reason for *why* your organization exists.
    - This should be clear, public, and undeniable to anyone connected with your business from the inside or outside—employees, customers, vendors, shareholders, and investors.
    - It should start with a CEO or founder and cascade down to the front lines of your business with sincere confirmation at every level.
2. Ensure that all stakeholders understand the purpose of your organization.
    - In an ideal world, everyone connected to your business—employees, contractors, vendors, customers, shareholders, and investors—would be able to recite your purpose statement verbatim.
3. Ensure all stakeholders believe in and are passionate about the purpose of your organization.
    - In an ideal world, everyone connected to your business—employees, contractors, vendors, customers, shareholders, and investors—would actively speak about, promote, and get others excited about helping to fulfill your organization's purpose.

Success Begins with Alignment

If you want to fulfill your organization's purpose, you must surround yourself with people who believe what you believe. Not people who think like you, necessarily, but people who share your organization's common purpose and interests.

In Arizona, there is a storm chaser who works for a local news channel. In a recent advertisement, he said that when there is a storm kicking up, he can't not go—whether he is working or not. "No matter what is going on in my life, there is nothing I'd rather be doing," he admits. He loves chasing storms and can't help himself. He finds the work intoxicating. He considers himself on duty 24/7. His job is his life, and his life is his job. There is a clear alignment of purpose.

It would be unrealistic to expect all employees in your business to feel the way this storm chaser does about the work they do. The storm chaser is the ultimate example of life alignment. But the truth is that, if you can hire people who truly enjoy what they do so much that they would do it in their free time, you'll be finding a better match.

In most cases, those who work for charities are people with a strong purpose alignment. For example, if someone who loves animals works at a charity for animal well-being, she is more likely to focus on that area of life on and off the job. In 2012, I founded World Child Cancer USA to help children with cancer in the developing world. In 2014, I turned the chairman role over to Scott Howard, MD, a renowned child oncologist. He has dedicated his personal and professional life to treating and saving the lives of children with cancer. Because of his efforts and leadership, the charity has helped thousands of children around the world. Again, there is a perfect alignment between his own purpose and that of the charity. Despite this, it is important to note that a 100 percent alignment is rare and not always healthy. In these cases, it works. In others, such commitment can lead to burnout or regret later in life. Balance is key.

The storm chaser sees his life's purpose as chasing storms and sharing their power and beauty with others through pictures and video. He works for a news channel that shares his purpose of reporting on such weather conditions. There is ideal alignment. Like Howard, his engagement and contributions to his employer could not be greater. Simply put, he cares deeply about what he does, and the results are apparent.

The following six questions—and their answers—can help managers and organizations get a better understanding of who a candidate is and how good a fit that person may be for the role and within the team. These are questions you can use on online applications or, even better, in face-to-face interviews to gauge the personality and purpose of a new candidate. The questions have been designed to elicit unique and creative answers, ones that are more genuine and unprepared. Use them to get to know the person—and purpose—behind the resume.

Even if you don't ask any of these questions, I encourage you to ask things that are outside the normal scope of interview questions. Canned and expected questions will get you canned and prepared answers. You want and need to know more to ensure a better fit for your organization. This fit has a direct correlation with engagement and, ultimately, business results.

While it would be ideal to find candidates who align perfectly in all aspects with your job and organization, that is not a reasonable expectation. In life, the 80/20 rule usually applies across the board. If you can find 80 percent of what you are looking for, you are far ahead of the game. Statistics show that most American workers are not well aligned in their jobs, and 80 percent of workers worldwide are unhappy in their positions.[7] This is because candidates create resumes that they tailor to a company's job description. They say what they believe their interviewers will most want to hear.

It's a double-edged sword, though. On the company side, organizations paint an external façade and brand the position and company with an upgraded version of the truth. Instead of being honest about what they value and expect, they project what they wish they were. A company may tell candidates whatever it believes will entice them to take the job. After the candidate and company start working together, both soon discover who the other really is. Unfortunately, in many cases, the two don't like each other. When the honeymoon is over, they are left with a bad marriage. Following are the six questions to ask.

1. What Gets You Out of Bed in the Morning?

I once asked this question of a candidate, and he told me the alarm clock. Needless to say, that was the last answer I was looking for. What I want to hear is what really excites this person in life. What does he look forward to each day? What can he not wait to get up for? Think of Christmas morning as a kid, a birthday, or a trip to Disneyland. Search for that type of excitement coupled with an activity the person may now spend time doing as an adult.

2. If You Didn't Need Money, What Would You Do in Life?

This is a difficult question for a lot of people to internalize. Their first response is, "But I have a family to support! Plus, car payments, a mortgage, rent, and food and clothing to buy." This is where I ask people to get off life's treadmill for a moment and give themselves a gift—the gift of imagining what life could be like if they did what they loved every day and got paid for it.

For this question, people may need to imagine they won the lottery or found a money tree. The idea is to discover what a person is drawn to when she's freed from having to worry about receiving money for it.

Most everyone has to make money to support themselves and their loved ones. This is the way life works. But there are also many people who do what they love each day and get paid well for it. These people experience great abundance, fulfillment, and happiness in life. I have met many such people in my life and count myself among them.

While it is unrealistic to target a life where you do everything you love and get paid for it 100 percent of the time, just imagine how great life would be if you got at least 80 percent there. Unfortunately, some of life's little annoyances—like paying bills and preparing taxes—will probably never go away. But being able to do what you love every day and getting paid adequately for it? That would certainly make life much better.

3. When in Your Life Have You Been So Passionately Focused on an Activity That You Lost Track of Time?

For me, the answer to this question is when I am writing. I have been writing ever since I was a kid. It has always been a passion and love of mine. It could be 11 p.m. I could be tired and hungry. I could start writing and suddenly find that it is 4 a.m., and I haven't slept or eaten. It is like I entered a time warp.

A candidate's response to this type of a question is a huge road sign pointing to what they most love to do. It may not necessarily be what she is best at, but it is certainly what she loves most.

Think about your own response to this question. It could be building things, gardening, or playing with a child or pet. Whatever your response, it is a clue to what you could spend your days doing that you would not consider *work*. It's the thing that you can focus on without counting the hours until quitting time. Understanding this focus is crucial. It takes tasks from a nine-to-five job and makes them a purpose-driven mission of passion and fulfillment. It accelerates people engagement because the actions are a labor of love. Productivity skyrockets because people want to do more and more of what they love most.

4. What Are You Most Interested In?

Have you ever been speaking to someone and touched upon a subject he was passionate about? What happened? Most likely, the person's eyes lit up, his speech quickened, his energy became elevated, his posture improved, and he may have even pulled himself forward in his seat. When someone is truly excited about a topic, it's obvious.

This same principle applies when you are interviewing a candidate. When you ask someone to talk about what he loves most, he undergoes a noticeable change. Just ask this question and watch what happens. It is truly social magic.

In your quest to peek behind the façade of rehearsed interview answers, this question will help break away most masks. You want to hire people who love what they do, not just someone who needs a job.

The problem remains that many people look for jobs because they need money, instead of looking for what they love to do and trying to get paid for it. As I mentioned earlier, pay alone is not a strong engagement factor. Employees can always get offered more money to work somewhere else.

5. What Do You Want Others to Remember You For?

This is the legacy question. Tragically, most people only start to question their lives when it is already too late—on their deathbeds. They have regrets. "I should have . . . What if I had done . . . I always wanted to do this . . . I could have made such a difference doing . . ." It is a shame.

This fifth question gives candidates an opportunity to travel forward in time and look back, to think about the end of their lives perhaps halfway through it, or even earlier. This is a powerful question and exercise—again, it delivers an opportunity to look at the heart and soul of a prospective candidate. Does this job really align with her desires, passions, and hopes? The closer the alignment, the higher the level of engagement and job satisfaction, and the better the output and the positive business outcomes will be.

6. What Was the Purpose of Your Last Organization? Did It Inspire You—and Why or Why Not?

Unless this is the interviewee's first job, answers to this last question can tell you a number of things about the candidate: whether she's attuned to purpose, an optimist or a pessimist, and whether she can articulate what inspired her and why. This helps focus the candidate on the bigger picture of organizational purpose.

Few organizations understand the concept of purpose alignment in recruiting better than Y Scouts. Founded in 2012 by Max Hansen and Brian Mohr, it is a purpose-based leadership search firm. I have been an advisor and friend to them from the beginning.

Y Scouts' process is truly innovative and disruptive in the recruiting space. Instead of candidates applying for positions that are posted on the site, interested individuals join Y Scouts' community online without the knowledge of any potential opportunities. From there, those selected are put through a rigorous life purpose assessment to determine the roles/organizations they would be best suited for and love most. On the organization's side, a similar process occurs, helping leaders within the organization identify and understand what candidate profiles would help move their organizational purpose forward. Neither party is aware of the other at this stage. Only once an organizational purpose and candidate alignment are identified are both parties introduced.

"Gone are the days when headhunting meant finding the best resume in a blue suit to fit that corner office. Today, finding an exceptional leader means aligning on not only performance, but purpose," Y Scouts insists.

"In early 2012, I teamed up with Max Hansen and Brett Farmiloe to build a company that would allow anyone to connect, to align, and to build a career based on something other than just financial rewards," Mohr explains.

"With more than 70 percent of the workforce disengaged in their work, we knew there had to be a better way to help leaders and companies connect in the recruitment process. Bad leadership is the number-one reason for poor engagement, and we believe purpose-driven leadership will reverse that trend. In fact, we've witnessed awe-inspiring transformations that prove purpose is not just an ideology, but a bottom-line strategy and a competitive advantage. The highest currency in today's employment market is meaningful work, not just a paycheck," Mohr concludes.

Being able to articulate your organizational purpose is key to recruiting the right people for your company. Organizations with a strong sense of purpose talk about it on their websites, showcase it in printed materials, in advertisements, and on the walls of their offices, and frequently speak about it at all levels of their organization. The other piece of the puzzle is finding the candidates who are intrinsically attracted to and inspired by your purpose. Understanding where you come from and what you're trying to achieve as an organization, as well as building teams who believe in that purpose and are driven by it, will boost your company's success in metrics across the board.

Chapter Questions

If you are struggling to identify your organization's purpose—why it was started in the first place—take a moment now to imagine a world without your organization. Then ask yourself the following questions.

- What would the world be like if my organization disappeared today?
- What would be missing from the world? What void would it leave?
- How would our customers suffer? What would they be missing?

Now ask the same questions of those who work for you, as well as of customers of your business. These questions and their answers will quickly illuminate the road to discovering, confirming, drafting, and communicating your organizational purpose statement.

Notes

1. *Merriam-Webster Dictionary.* s.v. "purpose." www.merriam-webster.com/dictionary/.
2. Goodreads, s.v. "Artistotle." www.goodreads.com/quotes/431261-where-your-talents-and-the-needs-of-the-world-cross.

3. John Nemo. "What a NASA Janitor Can Teach us About Living a Bigger Life." *The Business Journals*, December 23, 2014. www.bizjournals.com/bizjournals/how-to/growth-strategies/2014/12/what-a-nasa-janitor-can-teach-us.html.
4. Daniel Pink. *Drive*. New York: Riverhead Books, April 5, 2011, Chapters 2 and 2A.
5. Donna Vitale. *Culture of Purpose: A Business Imperative 3*. New York: Deloitte, 2013.
6. Walmart. "Our Purpose." June 16, 2013. http://news.walmart.com/media-library/videos/youtube/our-purpose-ai3sofjq9xw.
7. Alyson Shontell. "80% Hate Their Jobs—But Should You Choose a Passion or a Paycheck?" *Business Insider*, October 4, 2010. www.businessinsider.com/what-do-you-do-when-you-hate-your-job-2010-10.

CHAPTER 2

Finding Your Way

Your present circumstances don't determine where you can go; they merely determine where you start.

—Nido Qubein

Do you know why your organization exists? Why was it started in the first place? What does the future vision of your organization look like? What day-to-day actions do you and other employees need to take to fulfill your organization's purpose? If you don't know, you are not alone.

Many organizations, big and small, do not know the foundation that drives their people engagement and business results. Instead, they turn to their profit-and-loss statements, trying to drive business results based on financial forecasts, budgets, and targets. But have you discovered the disconnect? Business success is due to the innovation and perseverance of people. Most people don't jump out of bed every morning with a burning desire to add $5 or $10 million to their employer's top or bottom line. They jump out of bed for something bigger and more important to them. To bridge the gap, you need to develop a clear understanding of *why* an organization exists, *where* it is going, and *what* needs to happen to get there—so it can fulfill its purpose.

Knowing *why*, seeing *where*, and doing *what* create a foundation that sparks high levels of people engagement (from both employees and customers), loyalty, and business results. Defining and communicating this critical information can be the difference between exceptional success and catastrophic failure.

Your organization's *why* is its purpose—why it was started in the first place, beyond making money.

Your organization's *where* is its vision—where it is going and what it will look like when it arrives.

Your organization's *what* is its mission—what it needs to do day to day to fulfill its purpose.

How an organization engages a workforce around its *why*, *where*, and *what* is key. In order to achieve maximum engagement from employees, contractors, vendors, and customers, there must be a clear understanding of all three. Let's discuss each now in detail. This discussion represents the first foundational step in your journey.

Why

If you've ever started or run your own business, you will know that making easy money is not usually the impetus for this decision. Even in the best-case scenarios, making money in your own business is difficult. The rewards can be great, but the risks and hard work are even greater. If you simply need to make money, getting a job is much easier.

Organizations are started for a bigger reason than money. They are started because the owners or founders want to impact society, their community, or customers in a certain way. They have a passion for what they are about to undertake. They might see a gap in the market and deliver a solution. Or they might be reacting to a situation where they see a positive opportunity. Either way, a passion that's uniquely their own inspires most founders to go into business. Lacking that, and considering the hard work connected to running a business, it's hard to imagine many businesses starting as mere vehicles to generate profits.

Purpose is universal at the beginning: every company has one. But the problem with purpose is that, over time, organizations forget why they were started in the first place. Leaders change. Board members come and go. Teams shift, and the culture evolves. As companies get larger, they start chasing their profits and losses instead of pursuing the fulfillment of the organization's original reason for existing.

It is a given that every commercial organization needs to deliver a strong profit-and-loss statement. But if the focus is solely on trying to sell more for less, people engagement will be low and results will ultimately fall short. Commitment, loyalty, and long-term sustainability come from focusing on the fulfillment of the organization's purpose to achieve sales and profits. For most leaders, this requires changing the way they think about their business. It means shifting their focus to address the cause of real success and not the symptom of bringing in more sales and profits. Focusing unduly on the symptoms instead of the root cause leads to low engagement and high turnover. You've heard of businesses "beating people to sell more and drive costs down"—you don't want to be like them. In most cases, they are not fun places to work, and, even if they achieve short-term gains, their results soon stagnate.

Dan Henkle, president of Gap Foundation and SVP of global sustainability at Gap Inc., holds purpose dear. In 1969, Gap opened its first store because, as the story goes, Don Fisher—cofounder with his wife Doris—couldn't find a pair of jeans that fit. That was the moment that ignited his passion. His purpose—"to make it easier to find a pair of jeans and a commitment to do more"—ended up transforming retail.

Since the company's humble beginnings on Ocean Avenue in San Francisco, Gap went public, established a charity arm called Gap Foundation, acquired Banana Republic, Athleta, and Intermix, introduced GapKids, went global, birthed Old Navy, released an industry-leading annual corporate social responsibility report, raised the minimum hourly wage for sixty thousand U.S. employees, became the first Fortune 500 company to analyze and publicly share that women and men are paid equally for equal work, and became an iconic clothing brand around the world. Gap's purpose is being fulfilled because the company has not lost sight of what Fisher set out to do. The company's results prove it, too. Its clothing is available in ninety countries worldwide through thirty-three hundred company-operated stores, almost four hundred franchise stores, and several e-commerce sites.

Don Fisher's motto was always, "We need to do more than sell clothes." "This has been the driver of our greater good," says Henkle, a twenty-five-year employee. "We focus on how we connect our business to society and play our part. It's been a good guiding mantra for employees and helped us as we expanded into other countries and when sourcing for our business."

Gap's purpose and its supporting values play an important role in its leadership stances on corporate and social issues. In 2014, Gap did an analysis on its gender pay gap and became the first company to publicly commit to equal pay for equal work. Gap's bold move inspired other companies to be more transparent in their compensation practices. Gap received so much attention for its leadership position on pay equity that Henkle was invited to join a panel with Hillary Clinton to discuss the issue. "It's a good example of where we've taken a leadership role and how it's played a part in moving things in society forward," Henkle highlights.

Gap's *why* impacts everything it does, from how it hires, retains, and develops people to how it makes, distributes, and sells its products. Purpose is the path the company has chosen or that has chosen it. Another example is Gap's Personal Advancement Career Enhancement program (PACE). The program was rolled out first in its supply chain, which is about 80 percent female. The PACE program's intention is to educate people and enhance their career advancement opportunities and life skills. Gap started in its supply chain because it wanted to positively impact more women in the workforce. In 2015, it made a commitment to take the program to one million women by 2020—going beyond its workforce to advance women's lives and careers around the world. Yet another example is Gap's This Way Ahead program, which connects low-income youth to the company's entry-level jobs and to career coaching.

Where

Where relates to your organization's future vision, explained by where you are going and what things will look like when you get there. Leaders' ability to paint a clear and colorful picture of your organization's future drives people engagement, retention, and meaning.

Growing up in Santa Monica, California, I spent a good deal of my early childhood at Griffith Park with my parents. I rode the horses, ran on the grass, climbed play structures, and went round and round on the park's carousel. If you visit the park today, you will still see shadows of its famous past. In fact, one of the park benches still in existence is a place where Walt Disney sat in the 1940s watching his children ride the very same merry-go-round I enjoyed.

On a park bench surrounding this nearly turn-of-the-century carousel, Disney had a vision of a place where children and parents could play together. He was tired of being a bystander to all the fun his children were having without him. His vision was Disneyland.

Back in the 1950s, the idea of a $17 million amusement park built on 160 acres around an animated mouse may have seemed outlandish. Most amusement parks in those days were better suited to alcohol, drugs, and prostitution than to children and families. Despite the odds stacked against him, Disney began sharing his vision with others. His objective was to get others to see what he saw. It worked. Today the Walt Disney Company is one of the largest entertainment conglomerates in the world.

Disney was a true visionary in every sense of the word. He knew where he wanted and needed to go and was able to share his vision effectively with others so they could see it too. Walt believed that if you can see it, you can achieve it. Words that don't paint pictures fall flat. Journeys and organizations without visions for the future quickly lose focus and fall apart.

If your people and customers can't see where you are trying to go, it is impossible for them to help you get there. Your organization's *where* connects the lines on the map from where you are today to the place you're working to arrive in the future. Without it, your organization will be directionless and end up working on the wrong things. When the vision is lost, your business can take off in different and conflicting directions.

What

What is defined by the specific things you do each day that feed your purpose and ultimately drive your organization to where you want and need to go. The key part of understanding what you do is helping your people see the alignment between every action they take during their day and the larger purpose of your organization. This alignment not only creates meaningful work but also accelerates people engagement and drives business results that fulfill your purpose and move you toward your vision. It is imperative that all the people in your business understand the alignment of what they do connected to the bigger picture of your organization. To the contrary, if you are doing lots of work in your business that has no connection to your larger purpose, you are wasting both money and resources. Everything you do in your business should ultimately feed your purpose. If it does not, you should stop doing it.

Imagine if . . .

> Everything your people did had meaning and purpose for them and your organization.
>
> People always knew what to do and where to focus their efforts because of a specific connection to a common purpose and clear vision.

How much more engaged and productive would they be? How much more successful would your organization be?

Now imagine that Walt Disney had retained his vision of creating a family-friendly amusement park but had everyone on his team focused on ways to make the biggest profit from each ticket sale instead of how to bring Mickey Mouse and Walt Disney's imagination to life at Disneyland. Would Disney have grown into the company we know and love today?

Or imagine that the founders of the Gap had focused on sourcing the most inexpensive denim for their jeans to maximize profits instead of focusing on responsibly helping people look and feel good in their wardrobe? Would Gap's clothes be as prolific as they are today?

When I lived in England, my family and I visited Oxford Castle. On our tour, I saw the Crank Machine, a tool of physical and psychological punishment utilized in the nineteenth-century prison system.

As the name implies, the Crank Machine has a handle that can be turned, or "cranked." This handle is connected to nothing but pulleys and brakes, making turning it extremely difficult. Think about the toughest spinning class you've ever attended—and then some. With a stationary bike you don't go anywhere, but you can achieve an effective and balanced workout. The Crank Machine was tied to nothing productive. As a form of punishment, prisoners were compelled to turn it up to fifteen thousand times a day in their jail cell. The Crank Machine's sole purpose was to break the will of prisoners—to extinguish their purpose and engagement in life.

While my Crank Machine example is admittedly extreme, modern organizational tasks perceived to have little or no value can have a similar negative impact on people. The very act of doing such work could demotivate and punish a person who wants to make a difference in your organization.

Studies show nothing is more disengaging than doing work without perceived value, even if you are paid well for it. Connecting the work your people do to a shared organizational purpose and clear vision accelerates people engagement and drives profits.

In fact, getting your *why*, *where*, and *what* right can produce a high level of self-management in your organization, too. If people know why your organization exists, where it is going, and what they need to do daily to get there, they will need less management to get the job done.

Art of Self-Management

Ant colonies—sometimes numbering in the billions—don't need centralized leadership because they embrace the philosophy of self-management.[1] Ants are self-managed. They use triggers and interactions in their local environments to independently guide their work decisions. This is possible because all ants embrace a common purpose and only perform work that helps fulfill it.

Ant colony organization is so advanced, effective, and purpose-driven that notable companies like Southwest Airlines, Air Liquide, and others have used ants' patterns of behavior to solve complex business challenges.

Ants self-manage based on the rhythms and connections in their environment. In a human equivalent, these connections could be the rate at which others are working nearby and the environmental triggers that are seen or heard in their area. Providing there is common purpose for every person involved in the task, no defined leadership is needed to accomplish it. Successful examples of this self-managed model can be found in thriving organizations like W. L. Gore & Associates, Zappos, The Morning Star Company, and Treehouse.

The following are some examples of *why*, *where*, and *what* statements I have recently worked on in the automotive and banking industries. They will help guide you in your thinking as you define or refine the first steps of your journey to build the foundation in which Purpose Meets Execution rests.

Many traditional industries and organizations struggle to define their *why*, *where*, and *what*. However, the tide is shifting fast. Industries like the auto care and banking industries are two great examples. Many people think of the auto care industry as made up of nothing more than companies that sell wiper blades, washer fluid, or lug nuts for tires. Because of this, this $500 billion industry has struggled to attract new talent to its industry—talent looking for a higher purpose. The truth is that the industry is intensely purpose-driven. Speaking at auto care's AAPEX 2015 event, one of the largest annual conventions in Las Vegas, I defined the industry's *why*, *where*, and *what* in my keynote as follows.

Auto Care Industry

Why: To keep the world moving.

Imagine if the auto care industry disappeared today. Hundreds of thousands of people could not get to work, take their kids to school, go on family holidays, or generally get from point A to point B. This industry literally keeps the world moving.

Where: To serve every vehicle on the road.

This vision transcends all innovation moving forward. Presenting at several auto care events, I discovered the industry's focus on moving from servicing gasoline cars to electric vehicles. The purpose to keep the world moving remains consistent; it moves from old to new technology and can even encompass something as futuristic as flying cars.

What: To provide parts and services to make vehicles last longer, perform better, and keep drivers safe.

What the auto care industry does every day under this definition feeds its purpose—its *why—and* ultimately its *where.*

Banking Industry

Why: To improve life for individuals, families, organizations, and communities through financial services.

Imagine a world without the banking industry. You could almost envision people sleeping on mattresses balanced atop piles of cash. Without this industry, people would have no place to safely hold their money and help them invest, buy homes, or plan for their family's future. Organizations would not be able to gain the needed funds to allow their businesses to get through tough times or succeed. Communities would struggle to fund needed development projects, and the world would generally lack a financial infrastructure to facilitate trade. The banking industry's purpose is quite strong, despite a perception by some that they are simply money handlers.

> *Where*: To effectively serve and delight every customer in the financial services sector.

As in the auto care industry, this vision transcends all forms of economic and financial trade and services. It could encompass cash, credit, bitcoins, or any other form of electronic currency. It's a sustainable vision and one people working for your organization, as well as customers, can connect with.

> *What*: To provide the right financial services solutions for customers to empower them to achieve their goals and objectives.

The day-to-day actions of the banking industry under this definition feed the purpose and drive the industry forward toward its vision.

The auto care and banking industries are two prime examples of a shift in thinking about business and success in the world today and into the future. This three-part focus is helping organizations attract both younger and older-generation talent. Plus, it helps the people working for your organization and customers to focus on the right things in order to accelerate engagement and drive profits.

Defining your organization's *why*, *where*, and *what* is absolutely critical to ensuring that you are doing the right things to get where you want to go in the future and achieve the highest level of success and sustainability possible.

Chapter Questions

To ensure that your organization or industry is aligned and has clarity around its *why*, *where*, and *what*, ask and answer the following questions.

If you or the people working for your organization answer no to any of the following questions, you need to spend time defining, validating, and communicating your organization's *why*, *where*, and *what*. Organizations that fail to establish a strong foundation based on these three principles struggle to achieve the results they desire and suffer from instability. Plus, based on an evolving workforce, they have a much higher risk of extinction from failing to attract and retain the best of the next-generation workforce.

- Do I know and believe in my organization's *why*, *where*, and *what*?
- Do the people working for my organization know and believe in my company's *why*, *where*, and *what*?
- Do our *why, where*, and *what* align with our daily tasks and long-term objectives?

Note

1. "Ant Colonies: Social Organization Without a Director?" *Serendip Studio*. http://serendip.brynmawr.edu/complexity/models/antcolonies/page2.html.

CHAPTER 3

Avoiding the Pitfalls of Purpose

The most successful people in life are the ones who settle their critical issues early and manage them daily.

—John C. Maxwell

Running a business with purpose is essential to achieving exceptional results, but like all affairs that involve the heart, certain red flags may crop up along the way. Ignoring them can endanger your mission. Because you are striving for a higher level of people engagement than traditional organizations achieve, you need to look out for and avoid specific things: focusing too much on purpose, not profit; burnout; lack of leadership; a CEO-centered mindset; and the disenchanted customer. Each on its own or all five together can be devastating to an organization trying to build a culture of purpose. They can hinder the chance that you will be able to make a real difference to your customers, your community, and the world.

For Purpose—Not Profit

Running a commercial purpose-driven organization is not the same as operating a traditional charity. In all commercial enterprises, profits are a requirement for sustainability. Without profit, your organization will ultimately not be able to impact anyone or anything, much less stay in business. Making money requires strong and effective execution to get the right things done and deliver lasting business outcomes.

Even charities are not exempt from effective business execution. Goodwill Industries International, the eighty-year-old charity, suddenly closed sixteen Toronto-area stores and ten donation centers in early 2016.[1] The move shocked the community, and the CEO of Goodwill Industries of Toronto, Eastern, Central, and Northern Ontario (TECNO) resigned shortly after. Though Goodwill was striving to do good in the community, it eventually went bankrupt. Goodwill's purpose is not only to provide clothing and household goods for needy families but also to help provide jobs for the community. Its focus includes employing people who have physical and mental disabilities. Due to a lack of successful business execution, the organization was not only unable to help more people find jobs, but it ultimately had to let hundreds of workers in its centers go. Good intentions alone don't feed necessary financial results.

Many purpose-driven organizations tend to come out of the gate thinking like a traditional charity. They are so focused on the cause that they forget what they need to do to fulfill their purpose. The only way to institute real change is to sustain your organization through profits. If you have to shut down because you have been unable to deliver what needs to be delivered, you fail across the board. If you are trying to change the world in some way but lose money on every product you sell, you will eventually run out of funds and go out of business. You won't be able to effect meaningful change—even though that was your purpose in the first place.

Additionally, a purpose-driven organization that fails to manage an effective business model and strategy tends to run a very high-cost business. It can spend money blindly, fail to manage inventory, and burn through cash at a high rate in the name of "purpose"—something bigger than money. In contrast, organizations that balance their purpose with effective business execution manage their expense line in a healthier manner. It is dangerous to believe that people, communities, and society will continue to funnel funds and investment into something that they believe in strongly but that fails to deliver the needed business outcomes over the long term. At some point, the organization must become sustainable. It is irresponsible not to. Investors and followers will become disheartened when they feel the burden of the organization's success and purpose falls entirely on their shoulders. It is easy for organizations to burn through cash in an effort to move their purpose forward, but only the organizations that can remain profitable through effective business execution will survive to fulfill their purpose in a meaningful way.

If you run a commercial business of any kind, being purpose-driven requires that you make and manage money. The more you make and the better you manage it, the more of a difference your organization will be able to deliver. Making money is not an ugly concept in the corporate purpose movement; it is an essential part of it.

Burnout

When you hire people who truly believe in and align with your organization's purpose, they tend to work harder. This is both good and bad. The good side is obvious. The bad is often wrongly dismissed with comments that cast doubt on a person's dedication to the organization. Early in my corporate career, a manager leaving on vacation said to me, "Unless my house is burning down, don't contact me." I was taken aback by his brazen disinterest in work while he vacationed. "This guy is not going to last long," I thought. Instead, it turned out to be a key leadership lesson for me.

The pitfall of burnout is real, and it costs organizations a substantial amount of money and business disruption. It manifests itself in low people engagement, high turnover, poor product quality, health-related leave, and increased insurance premiums. People report losing sleep over their work, missing important family events, and disregarding other priorities. They can become myopic in their focus on what they are doing—which may seem good. However, this can quickly sour when someone's personal life, health, or well-being start falling apart. Engagement will quickly decline, people will become unhappy, and, despite their belief in and dedication to your organization, they will eventually leave. This will not only cost your business good talent, it will cause disruption to your customers and your product flow and force you to spend more time, money, and resources to hire and train new people.

It is important that organizations actively balance the dedication that like-minded people show and those peoples' personal lives. Creating a healthy balance stimulates increased engagement and sustainable personal and business results. You want people to work hard, but you don't want them to ultimately regret their dedication to your business, cause, or purpose. Once you have disciples, you want to keep them engaged, happy, and producing at a high level. Finding like-minded people for your business is critical to achieving exceptional results, but even more important is being able to retain them in the long run. High turnover can be a significant problem in purpose-driven organizations that fail to actively manage work–life integration for their people. This problem is sometimes so extreme that it can even force people to leave their own business. David Niu, the founder of TINYhr and author of *Careercation*, left his own thriving enterprise because he overworked himself and lost track of other important parts of his life, like his family.

Some ways to actively manage this integration include offering unlimited paid time off, instituting business shutdown periods, celebrating time off, and enforcing e-mail blackout periods. The best way, however, is still leadership by example. A study by Kelton Research commissioned by the Radisson hotel chain indicates that nearly half of the total American workforce doesn't use all of their allotted vacation days.[2] From my experience leading HR functions at mid-sized to large organizations, I can confirm that the core offenders are managers and leaders.

It is disingenuous for a leader to tell someone to stop working and take a vacation or recover from an illness, only to show up to work a week later coughing and sneezing. I have heard leaders boast about not taking a vacation in ten years. Under these leaders, people feel they are not allowed to fully unplug, despite being encouraged to do so. As with all aspects of effective leadership, walking the talk is the only way to create lasting change. If leaders take time off, their reports will feel empowered to do so, too.

Lack of Leadership

Purpose-based organizations tend to attract and hire very smart and driven people. As the organization grows, these people can believe that they can do any role well, even leading people, because they are so passionate about the organization's purpose. There is a tendency to promote great individual contributors loyal to the cause into leadership and management roles without any assessment or even a discussion to determine whether they will be good people leaders. In most cases, there is not even a day of training that accompanies this significant promotion. These people are tossed into the leadership waters to sink or swim. In many cases, they sink as they fail to engage those around them. Sadly, it is only when the organization starts to face substantial business troubles that these people get called out to take the blame for the business's challenges. In most cases, it is the business's fault for placing a person in a role where he can't win, either because he lacks the natural talent to be a leader or because he simply never received the training or support to do the job effectively.

It's ironic to promote someone from an individual contributor role—based on his success in that role—to a management or leadership role: the very things that made that person successful as an individual contributor may be the traits that work against her as a manger or leader. A salesperson who is successful selling products most likely enjoys the buzz of closing a deal or getting the personal recognition for achieving her numbers. A leader or manager of salespeople needs to be able to step back and help people achieve the sales and recognition. The very talents a person brought to the table in direct sales need to be mostly suppressed if she is to be an effective leader in this area.

If you have the natural ability, leadership may come easily. If you are best suited as a salesperson, however, you will end up doing the work rather than managing it, frustrating and disengaging the people on your team. Such "leaders" will turn to what they know and do best—selling—not managing or leading. The same applies for an engineer who may love tinkering, building, and creating things. If you move him into a leadership role without understanding whether he has a talent or passion for developing others, he will not engage those working for him and may become frustrated and ultimately fail. Organizations spend a lot of time, money, and resources trying to find the right people to work in their organizations. If you have poor leaders or people who should not be in leadership or management roles, you may lose your pool of talent. People don't leave organizations—they leave managers, despite their connection or alignment to a purpose.

Another challenge that accompanies a lack of leadership is that hiring managers may think that being purpose-driven means hiring people who all think like them. This is a dangerous practice and creates what is known as groupthink: the practice of thinking or making decisions as a group in a way that discourages creativity or individual responsibility.[3] Instead, organizations need to look for diverse thinkers who also align with their purpose.

CEO-centered Mindset

In purpose-driven organizations, it is quite common for founders or CEOs to center their movement around themselves rather than build the purpose into the organizational DNA of the company. Because they care so much about what they're trying to do, they feel the need to control every aspect of what goes on in the organization or to be involved in every detail. Doing this creates an unsustainable organization. The founder or CEO becomes a crutch for the organization, and, over time, this builds a lack of self-reliance. When an organization or movement is built around one person, the absence of that person puts the entire organization and its purpose at risk.

The story of Edwin H. Land, cofounder of Polaroid, is a case in point. Land was the center of everything at Polaroid.[4] As his organization grew, Land had teams of people working in shifts at his side. As one team wore out, the next team rotated in to continue the work. Land was at the core of everything at Polaroid and was even accused of wearing the same clothing for eighteen consecutive days because he refused to take a break. As brilliant as Land was, he failed to develop a sustainable organization. Subsequently, his ill equipped and undeveloped successors mismanaged the company, and the once great organization headed into a downward spiral. In his 2012 book, *Instant: The Story of Polaroid*, Christopher Bonanos notes that Polaroid's competitor Kodak referred to Land's company as "He" instead of Polaroid. In October 2001, Polaroid declared bankruptcy.

Effective founders and CEOs build organizations engrained with knowledge, experience, leadership, and empowerment. The organization can survive without such CEOs. This is what being truly sustainable means. An organization must be able to function in whole or part without relying on a single individual.

A leader is not doing her followers, boss, or organization any favors by building a team that can't function without her. Leaders have a duty of care to teach their followers to fish instead of fishing for them. At day's end, the true test of effective leadership manifests itself when a leader is absent.

The one thing that all effective leaders do is make themselves redundant so they can move on to even greater challenges and help more people, knowing that the team or organization they built will flourish and carry on fulfilling its purpose.

The Disenchanted Customer

A strong organizational purpose may drive customer buying decisions despite initial product quality issues, but that advantage won't last forever. There comes a time in the evolution and maturity of a business when customers and investors expect more. If you fail to deliver on these expectations, people will eventually become disenchanted and stop buying your products. Customer and investor loyalty to a fault is good and necessary for some start-ups, however, especially those marketing and selling disruptive technology.[5]

Harvard Business School professor Clayton M. Christensen introduced and defined disruptive technology in his 1997 best-selling book, titled *The Innovator's Dilemma (Management of Innovation and Change)*, as an emerging technology that unexpectedly displaces an established one. These are new technologies that still lack refinement, often have performance problems, are known only to a limited public, and might not yet have a proven practical application. They are innovations that need time and, in most cases, an intensive amount of resources to grow into something valuable to society. Remote health monitoring, mobile banking, virtual reality, advanced robotics, and the modern electric car are a few examples. Despite these allowances, there comes a time when an organization must make good by its customers and deliver the products and services they promise at a high quality. Customers can be forgiving—but they won't forgive forever.

Chapter Questions

To avoid the potential pitfalls of a purpose-driven organizational culture, ask and answer the following questions. Your responses will shed light on how prepared you are to deal with and avoid problems as you develop or sustain high engagement, high performance, and a purpose-focused culture.

Pitfall 1: For Purpose, Not Profit

- Is my organization currently making money, or on track to, in the short term? (If not, you may need to rethink the business strategy you are employing to fulfill your organization's purpose. Profit is essential to your success.)

Pitfall 2: Burnout

- Is my organization's people turnover high? (If so, check your industry averages and work to make improvements on that benchmark.)

- If turnover is high, why are people leaving? What is the cost to my organization? How can I address it in the short and long term?

Pitfall 3: Lack of Leadership

- Are the people in leadership and management roles at my organization best suited for those positions and playing to their strengths?
- Does my organization have a process in place to assess future leaders and evaluate the ones currently in such roles?

To assess whether leaders, or anyone else in your organization, are in the right roles, ask them the following questions:

- What do you believe you do best?
- What do you do in life where you get the most positive feedback?
- What do you do in life where you get the most negative feedback?
- To those who work with the person in question, pose the following question: What do you believe this person does best?

The insights gained from the answers to these questions will give you an assessment of the strengths of the people in your organization and their correct placement to add maximum organizational value.

Pitfall 4: CEO-centered Mindset

- If I, my leader, or my CEO quit today, would my team/organization continue to be successful and grow, with minimal long-term disruption?

Pitfall 5: The Disenchanted Customer

- Does my organization receive an excessive number of customer complaints? (If you answer yes to this question, you are heading down a dangerous path of losing customers, missing referrals, and creating a poor brand reputation. Customers will give you "get out of jail free" cards for only a limited period of time.)

Notes

1. Janet Mcfarland, Jeff Gray, and Eric Andrew-Gee. "Charity Case: Why Goodwill's Failure in Toronto Was Anything but Sudden." *The Globe and Mail*, January 24, 2016. www.theglobeandmail.com/news/toronto/charity-case-why-goodwills-failure-in-toronto-was-anything-butsudden/article 28359611/.
2. Khadeeja Safdar. "Vacation Days Left Unused by Nearly Half of U.S. Workers: Report." *The Huffington Post*, April 12, 2012. www.huffingtonpost.com/2012/04/12/vacation-days-unused_n_1418517.html.
3. *Oxford Dictionary*.
4. Christopher Bonanos. *Instant: The Story of Polaroid*. New Haven, CT: Princeton Architectural Press. September 26, 2012.
5. Maria Fonseca. "Guide to 12 Disruptive Technologies." *Intelligent HQ*, March 2, 2014. www.intelligenthq.com/technology/12-disruptive-technologies/.

CHAPTER 4

Executional Excellence

Knowing is not enough; we must apply. Willing is not enough; we must do.

—Johann Wolfgang von Goethe

Nature is full of examples of executional excellence. Think about the magnificent albatross.[1] This feathered creature has the longest wingspan of any bird—up to eleven feet—and is one of the largest birds in the sky. Despite this, it can circle the globe in just forty-six days, traveling up to ten thousand miles in one session. In most cases, the purpose of its long flights is to locate its prey, squid in the ocean.

Because it weighs up to twenty-five pounds, flapping its wings to take off from the ground would take too much energy. The albatross would lose about half its body mass fueling such an endeavor. To effectively execute its remarkable flight logs, the albatross launches itself from ocean cliffs and rides the ocean winds, sometimes gliding for hours without rest or even a flap of its wings.

Like the albatross, organizations—large and small—that discover how to effectively execute to achieve their objectives can accomplish remarkable things. Those that don't ever discover effective execution can ultimately die, even if they have the strongest of purposes.

Will Tesla Change the World?

Before I started my role as head of global employee engagement at Tesla Motors, I was asked to prepare a presentation to about four hundred managers at a leadership off-site on my first day of employment. In the presentation, I included an aspiration for Tesla: "Be a market leader." I quickly learned that Tesla does not talk about being a "market leader" but rather about "changing the world." I had previously worked in two organizations—Stryker, a medical technologies firm, and JDA Software—where being a market leader was an intense focus. Despite still believing that being a market leader was the means to Tesla changing the world—to "accelerate the world's transition to sustainable transport"—I changed my slide heading to read, "Change the world."

My days at Tesla were filled with excitement, challenges, doubt, and interactions with some of the brightest minds in the world. It was like working in a futuristic fantasyland. There was an unbridled desire to push the boundaries of reality on a day-to-day basis.

Having spoken and written about organizational purpose for many years, I understood the importance of organizations striving to change the world for the better. It was important not only to me but to an evolving workforce of millions across the globe. I studied organizations like Whole Foods, IKEA, IDEO, and Commerce Bank—companies that were achieving that goal every day. I reviewed research that supported the fact that running a purpose-based organization was the single most powerful tool to driving top- and bottom-line growth.

But before working at Tesla, I had not focused much on how a business gets things done to truly make the world a better place—that is, how it executes in order to fulfill a purpose. During my eleven years at Stryker, the execution component was a given. Most of my global work for the organization involved engaging people around such execution. The infrastructure was already there and well established.

Tesla is a product of extremely fast growth without the benefit of a well established infrastructure or a people practices foundation. It grew before it was ready and was forced to play catch up. Growing from around 650 employees about six years ago to over thirty thousand at the time of writing this book, it races to continue to stabilize its foundation. The work I led successfully implementing a people engagement initiative across the organization was important, but it was just the tip of the iceberg in Tesla's journey to evolve its people practices in the right direction.

Tesla has had its fair share of market misses, product quality issues, financial shortfalls, government agency investigations, and stock volatility. Competition in the electric car market is heating up. If Tesla can't master executional excellence, it will hinder its ability to compete with established car manufacturers. Plus, its acquisition of SolarCity—seemingly pulling its immediate focus away from its core purpose of mass-producing affordable electric vehicles—may create further challenges in its quest to change the world.

A Need for Balance

The necessity for organizations to have and balance both purpose and execution came into focus for me. Purpose is the crucial foundation—execution, the catalyst to fulfill purpose.

It was clear to me that purpose-focused organizations that truly want to make a positive and lasting difference must sell more products, make more profit, reinvest into their business, and then hire and engage more like-minded people to grow and fulfill their purpose. To truly change the world, you must run a great business.

The airline industry is a grand example of highly effective execution. Despite the common fear of flying, millions of passengers move around the world safely every day. There is no acceptable ratio of planes that make it to their destination and those that don't. They all must get there safely. This purpose could never be fulfilled without executional excellence.

In live theater, too, no one would buy a seat for a well-written play or musical if the production team or performers couldn't execute to deliver a performance. Audience members want and expect a seamless exchange between purpose and execution. The better the balance, the better the press reviews, the more tickets are sold, the longer the show runs, and the more financially successful it is. The balance of purpose and execution ensures the best audience experience. There, the purpose is the subtext—the emotions below the dialogue—and the heart of everything going on in the theater, and execution is the catalyst to transport audiences to a new world. This is great theater, a complete suspension of disbelief because a balance of heart and mind is orchestrated.

Woody Allen, one of my favorite filmmakers, has been a part of an astonishing seventy-three films to date over his career.[2] Those he has written and directed have grossed more than $587 million, with an average of nearly $14 million per film. Allen is fulfilling his life's purpose through superb execution.

Even in an undertaking as seemingly simple as serving food, the same principle of execution applies. You can have the best marketing in the world, but if your food is bad or you can't get it to a customer's table in a timely manner, your restaurant will close.

Execution holds true in the retail industry, too; an exciting product doesn't matter if you can't deliver it when expected or needed or if it doesn't work when received. Execution is the industry's catalyst to fulfilling its purpose. The same principle applies to business-to-business entities.

The problem most organizations face when it comes to effective execution is that individuals and teams traditionally don't know or understand how the work they do each day connects to the organization's overall purpose. Their work lacks larger meaning. This translates into lower engagement and care for the work they do.

The Gallup organization did extensive research in this area.[3] Its findings show that there is a direct correlation between how people feel about the connection of their work to their employer's mission or purpose and employee retention, customer metrics, productivity, and profitability. Gallup concludes, "The best workplaces give their employees a sense of purpose, help them feel they belong, and enable them to make a difference."

In Dan Ariely's TED Talk, "What Makes Us Feel Good About Our Work?" he describes several experiments in which people were paid to do a simple task with decreasing amounts of compensation.[4] The groups were divided into three categories: those who had their work *acknowledged*; those who had their work *ignored*; and those who had their work *destroyed* after completion. In all the experiments, work that was ignored and work that was destroyed were held in basically the same regard in the mind of the task doers.

Additionally, those who felt their work had no meaning or offered no value were more likely to produce lower-quality work or cheat, despite the money they were making. Those who had their work acknowledged did more for less compensation, at a higher quality, and with a greater level of care. The basic human need to feel that one's work matters had a massive impact on how engaged people were in their jobs and how well they executed.

Making certain that every person in your business understands and sees the connection his work has to the bigger picture is key to high engagement and ensuring that the right things are getting done in your business. By creating a culture of executional excellence, you will build trust with both your internal and external stakeholders, who will believe you will keep promises and deliver what is expected.

Riders Must Ride: Harley-Davidson/AMF

Harley-Davidson's motto is "Live to Ride, Ride to Live."[5] Since 1903, the company has produced and sold its iconic motorcycles. It survived the Great Depression, numerous owners, periods of economic and product-quality challenges, and increased global competition. Today, it is the fifth-largest motorcycle manufacturer in the world, with owner clubs and events worldwide.

After riding motorcycles for the past twenty-five years and becoming a recent Harley owner myself, I connected to the brand's motto. For motorcyclists, buying a Harley is more about joining a family of riders than purchasing a new bike. However, as amazing as owning a Harley is, it means nothing if the machine doesn't work.

In 1969, American Machine and Foundry (AMF) bought Harley-Davidson and immediately went about cutting costs and workers and streamlining production. A labor strike ensued, and product quality plummeted. The motorcycles were expensive but inferior in performance, handling, and quality to Japanese bikes. Sales quickly declined, and Harley's brand was mocked with the motto, "Buy a Harley, buy the best—drive a mile, walk the rest."

In 1981, after nearly bankrupting the company, AMF sold Harley-Davidson to a group of investors for $80 million. Inventory became strictly controlled. Rather than trying to compete with intensifying Japanese competition, the new management decided to exploit the "retro" mystique of the bikes. The company started building motorcycles that captured the look and feel of Harley-Davidson's earlier machines and even incorporated owner customizations of that era. Many of the bikes' parts were outsourced to foreign manufacturers, and technical improvements were made. These changes brought about increased product quality, keeping Harley riders on the road. As a result, buyers returned to Harley, and sales began to roll in once again.

In 1990, the Harley "Fat Boy" was introduced, and the organization made its way back to a sales leader in the heavyweight bike market. Harley was once again executing at a high level, supporting its purpose to "fulfill dreams of personal freedom." Riders were able to "Live to Ride, Ride to Live." Balance had been restored, and so had the organization's successful trajectory.

Country Western Won't Keep This Restaurant in Its Saddle

After waiting tables for several years in New York City in tandem with my theater career, I learned firsthand about the importance of execution in the food services industry. Wait times, service levels, food quality and taste, and cleanliness all require strong execution if a restaurant is to deliver the optimum customer experience.

I was recently reminded of this balance when my family and I ate at a new Country Western restaurant near our home in Scottsdale, Arizona. The restaurant has a clear purpose to deliver a country western experience to its patrons. There is line dancing, a live country band, and healthy portions of BBQ on the menu.

Unfortunately, the food was just okay—and the service poor. The waitress left me, my wife, and our daughters unattended for some time. She couldn't answer questions about the menu, and our food came out staggered, forcing us to eat hot meals separately. When we finished, the table was not cleared. There was a lack of execution on just about every front. Despite a pleasant and smiley staff, and the fun we had on the dance floor after dinner, we will not return to the restaurant to dine.

Considering this restaurant's purpose, a lack of execution will almost ensure that it will never be fulfilled on a long-term or grand scale. With such poor execution, the benefit of return or word-of-mouth customers will be low, directly impacting top-line sales and bottom-line profits.

Had this restaurant lacked purpose, too, it is doubtful that it would have been open long enough for us to even eat at it. Its strong purpose will keep it afloat for a while but not forever, unless management and staff fix their execution problem.

Execution as a Matter of Life and Death

When you're flying fighter jets or going into combat, you must be prepared and execute correctly. Without proper execution, you are dead. Rob "Waldo" Waldman is a decorated fighter pilot and retired Air Force lieutenant colonel and combat veteran.[6] During active duty, he flew sixty-five combat missions. He is also an author, motivational speaker, leadership consultant, and the founder of The Wingman Foundation.

Waldman explains:

> It is critical as a fighter pilot and a soldier to prepare to make sure that you are doing whatever you need to do to go to battle and execute a plan. Attitude doesn't determine altitude, action determines altitude. It's fantastic if you're fired up, but if you don't supply the tactic to avoiding the missile, to hitting the target, to executing a great combat plan against adversaries trying to kill you, then your attitude is nothing. You must have both attitude and action—purpose and execution.

You have to love to fly, love the fight, love the thrill, and be passionate about being strapped into an F16 to be deployed. But most importantly, you have to be a skilled executor. The latter is the difference between life and death, victory and defeat.

For most people reading this book, business execution is not a life-or-death matter. Whether you're growing a business, developing a technology, or selling cars, failing to execute on a needed action will most likely not end a life. However, a consistent lack of execution in a business can mean the loss of jobs and income to feed, educate, and house families, and the deterioration of a person's livelihood. Poor or failed execution can mean the death of your organization and be equivalent to life or death for your people and even for customers who rely on your products to sustain their lives.

Organizational execution is not done in isolation, though. It requires a concerted effort, a one-team mentality. Waldman frequently refers to his wingmen, men and women in his formation who were depending on him to get his part of the job done. If he were to fail, it wouldn't affect only him but also the whole team and mission. His drive to execute tapped into something more than just himself. There was a bigger picture and more people at stake.

"It has to be about those that you're working with, those that you serve, those that need you to execute," Waldman insists.

Imagine you were flying together with a good friend in a squadron. She was getting shot at. Your job was to back her up and hers was to do the same for you. Your ability to execute would impact both of you, your team, your spouses, your children, your families, your friends, and your country. There is no room for error. You must commit and execute above all else. It should be obvious that an executional mindset that showed concern only for yourself would be deadly to all.

Waldman's guidance is squarely in line with my corporate experience. If organizations and teams fail to work together, silos form, internal competition outweighs external competition, business execution becomes self-serving, and barriers get in the way of optimal business results and success.

In the world of a fighter pilot, wingmen never wing it. "We never fly by the seat of our pants," Waldman says. One of the most critical things for fighter pilots is their focus on preparation for a mission. Planning, studying the threat, gathering intelligence, and being up-to-date with their processes and tactics are all essential steps. If they become complacent, if they are not current with their technology and processes, they are going to get shot down.

The best fighter pilots out there put in the time, sacrifice, and sweat to ensure they are prepared for the fight and executing on the right things. Leaders and managers of all organizations should take a leaf from their book. If you are not doing your homework, analyzing and studying your business, asking the right questions, and ensuring you are executing on the right things, you will ultimately fail. You can't afford to have people "winging it" in your business. There must be a clear plan of attack in every business action you take, at every level in your organization. You must understand your business, customers, strengths, weaknesses, opportunities, and threats.

"One of the things about being in a fighter squadron is that you could look to your left and right and say the important words in business and in life, which are, 'I need help,'" Waldman concludes. Creating trusting, wingman-like partnerships in your business is key to ensuring that everyone is supporting the ultimate purpose of the organization and executing on the right things to fulfill it.

When you're strapped in to an F16, you can't see your own most vulnerable position—the six o'clock on the face of a watch, which is right behind you. It's your blind spot and your biggest threat. Your wingmen become the eyes in the back of your head. Waldman refers to this as the principle of "Check-Six." Wingmen can see if you're leaking fuel, on fire, have structural damage, or if a missile is coming at you from the ground. Your wingmen have your back, and their wingmen have their backs. It's a force multiplier, and it increases what is known as situational awareness.

Situational awareness is key to ensuring that organizations are taking the right actions and executing on the right things to fulfill their purpose. Without eyes in the back of their heads, organizations tend to spend a lot of time working on non-value-added things. Most departments will have a long laundry list of must dos each year, but most of the items on the list have little ROI to the organization's bigger picture. In fact, in my experience, only about 10 percent of the things on an organization's to-do lists add true value to the business. Situational awareness helps eliminate this waste by having "wingmen" that keep you honest and focused. Is this work really adding value? Are you wasting important time? Are you missing an opportunity? What are your teammates working on? Are you aimed at your target? Is there a missile heading for you because you have been distracted with the wrong things? Are you focused on the right things? These are all questions that colleagues throughout your organization can help you answer—if you have a culture that embraces highly effective execution and communication. In air combat, these people include not only wingmen but those on the ground—intelligence officers, air traffic controllers, and refueling tankers. They all help you see and stay focused on the bigger picture. In an organization, everyone should serve as the eyes and ears for all colleagues.

In a fighter pilot squadron or any highly effective execution company, giving and receiving feedback, calling the threat and opportunity, improving the situational data, and maintaining open and honest communications are essential. Everyone needs to be open to honest feedback. This is

Waldman's concept of "never flying solo." After all, in a team situation, you're only as strong as your weakest link, and relying on others can build a complete picture you'd have never seen yourself.

A collaborative approach builds trusting teams, fosters core values and training, and improves human connection, caring, and appreciation. This in turn enables highly effective execution, allowing organizations to hit the target and live to fight another day.

Chapter Questions

Is your organization effectively executing at a high level? Ask and answer the following questions to determine where focus needs to be given.

- Do people inside and outside of my organization believe that we keep our promises?
- Do people know and understand how their day-to-day work connects to my organization's overall purpose?
- Do people feel they are adding value in their jobs and contributing to the success of my organization?
- Does my organization function as one team or in silos?
- Do I have wingmen at my organization?

Notes

1. Mollie Bloudoff-Indelicato. "How Giant Birds Can Fly Nearly 10,000 Miles in One Go." *National Geographic*, November 13, 2013. http://voices.nationalgeographic.com/2013/11/13/giant-birds-fly-nearly-10000-miles-in-one-go/.
2. Box Office Mojo, "Woody Allen." www.boxofficemojo.com/people/chart/?view=Director&id=woodallen.htm.
3. Gallup. "The Engaged Workplace." www.gallup.com/services/190118/engaged-workplace.aspx?gclid=CLS1yPzy084CFYdcfgodiIwCLw.

4. Dan Ariely. "What Makes Us Feel Good About Our Work?" *TED*, October 2012. www.ted.com/talks/dan_ariely_what_makes_us_feel_good_about_our_work.
5. Wikipedia. s.v. "Harley Davidson." https://en.wikipedia.org/wiki/Harley-Davidson.
6. Waldo Waldman. http://yourwingman.com.

CHAPTER 5

Where Purpose Meets Execution

You've got to think about big things while you're doing small things, so that all the small things go in the right direction.

—Alvin Toffler

Southwest Airlines' purpose is, "To connect people to what's important in their lives."[1] It does this "through friendly, reliable, and low-cost air travel." The airline's purpose and what it needs to execute on every day is clear. This purpose could not be fulfilled without executional excellence—especially since Southwest is in the business of air travel. An absolute balance must exist. If its planes can't get you safely from one destination to another, everyone loses.

Yelp's purpose is "to connect people with great local businesses."[2] Its clear purpose and ability to deliver on its promise attracted more than one hundred million visitors to its website in the first quarter of 2013. In the first quarter of 2016, Yelp had a monthly average of ninety million unique visitors to its platform. Its ability to effectively balance its organizational purpose and business execution has yielded remarkable results.

In Simon Sinek's 2011 book *Start with Why: How Great Leaders Inspire Everyone to Take Action*, he tells the story of Dr. Martin Luther King Jr.'s "I Have a Dream" speech on the National Mall in the summer of 1963.[3] A quarter of a million people attended. According to Sinek, the people who came to this unadvertised event did so not because they believed in Dr. King but because they rallied to his purpose. They made his purpose their own.

"It's not the products or services that bind a company together," Sinek concludes. "It's not size and might that make a company strong, it's the culture—the strong sense of beliefs and values that everyone, from the CEO to the receptionist, all share."

The only missing ingredient in the telling of this story is Dr. King's superb ability to execute. If you have ever watched the video of his speech, you will know firsthand the power and emotion of his delivery. Not only were Dr. King and his disciples able to execute at a high level to spread the word about the event—without the aid of the Internet—but the product he delivered was timely and of the highest quality. He brought his organization and talents to bear in order to deliver on a promise to those traveling to and attending the event. His speech moved millions and changed the course of history. This is the power of combining a clear purpose with executional excellence. Had all these people traveled to experience a weak and unprepared speech, little would have happened afterward.

O.C. Tanner: Creating Purpose

O.C. Tanner is an eighty-nine-year-old, privately held employee recognition and reward company headquartered in Salt Lake City, Utah. Its purpose is to develop strategic employee recognition and reward solutions that help people accomplish and appreciate great work.

O.C. Tanner is credited with pioneering the recognition industry. Its more than fifteen hundred employees deliver 4.2 million awards to 19 million employees worldwide annually. It was ranked two years running on the Fortune 100 Best Companies to Work For® list and maintains over a 99 percent on-time delivery record.

O.C. Tanner is a model of balance when it comes to purpose and execution. Obert Clark Tanner, the founder of O.C. Tanner, was the youngest of ten children. His purpose and interest in life always centered around human connection. He became a professor of philosophy and religious studies at Stanford and the University of Utah and held fellowships at Oxford and Cambridge. In the 1920s, after a discussion with a group of students who had just graduated from a seminary, he came to the conclusion that there was a missing component to recognizing important accomplishments in life. These students had worked extremely hard for many years, and all they received was a piece of paper for their efforts. Something more had to be done to commemorate the achievement. Tanner wanted to make graduation special, a big deal. He wanted graduates to feel proud of their accomplishment. He felt these moments in life deserved a pause for an opportunity to receive some type of a tangible representation of what they've achieved.

Tanner started designing and creating lapel pens in commemoration of seminary work. The pins were very well received. But Tanner knew that there had to be other people in the same boat in life—those who had accomplished great things but received little to no recognition for their achievements. Tanner started selling his pins to all kinds of associations whose members had accomplished something or achieved a certification.

On December 7, 1941, Tanner and his nephew and business partner, Norman Tanner, were skiing when they got news of the bombing of Pearl Harbor. Norman, the nephew, told Obert that he needed to leave the company and join the fight. During the course of World War II, Norman became a highly decorated pilot. His medals sparked an idea that would become the core of what O.C. Tanner is today.

Norman realized that the recognition he had received during his military career was not replicated in many organizations at the time. In fact, people of the postwar era were just happy to have paid jobs. Recognition for great work was not even an afterthought. You performed well or you lost your job. It was as simple as that. Despite this, employees were working extremely hard, achieving great things, building their careers, and creating big value for their employers. In most cases, all this went unrecognized and unappreciated. People were viewed as cogs in the industrial machine, not as individuals who would benefit and produce even greater results with some form of recognition or reward for exceptional work. Both Tanners felt people ought to be noticed, valued, and respected. They recognized that, without people, organizations can't grow or prosper. People need to be acknowledged, recognized, and valued.

O.C. Tanner shifted its focus to helping corporations recognize and value their people. They started with service awards to recognize employee loyalty and tenure. Whether awarded for ten, fifteen, or twenty years of service, O.C. Tanner's custom pins, for the first time ever, let companies pause and express appreciation. O.C. Tanner's purpose was clear, and it ignited an industry of employee recognition and rewards that had not existed before. That industry birthed the whole concept and realization that employee engagement matters to people and business results.

Even O.C. Tanner's thought leadership in the area of employee recognition and rewards would have meant nothing if it failed to execute and deliver on its customer promises. If employers were queued up to deliver recognition to their top performers but never received the products they ordered or were promised, O.C. Tanner would have been out of business—and its thought leadership would have perished.

Connecting Execution to Purpose

David Sturt, O.C. Tanner's executive vice president and the author of the *New York Times* best seller *Great Work: How to Make a Difference People Love*, recalls a company meeting where a financial goal of $500 million in revenue was announced. The CEO and then the sales leader both got up and talked about the goal and how great a milestone it would be for the company. "There was lots of rah-rah and rallying around it," Sturt recalls. After that, the daughter of the founder and current chair of the board, Carolyn Tanner Irish, spoke.

"Carolyn is a principled woman and very wise. I could see her watching the executive team getting all excited and wound up about the financial goal," Sturt shares. Then Irish got up and made some very profound observations:

> Five hundred million dollars seems important, and obviously our leaders are excited about it. They are right—we need good growth goals—but that isn't our ultimate goal. In fact, I don't recall seeing that big number, $500 million, on our strategy map, or in our mission statement. Our purpose isn't about reaching a certain sales number—it is about appreciating, recognizing, encouraging, and acknowledging people who do great work. That is why we do what we do. That is why we are expanding and growing throughout the world. If we take care of helping companies do this right and spread that around the world we'll achieve the financial goal.

"You could see people nodding in agreement in the meeting as they said to themselves, 'Yeah, she's right,'" Sturt remembers. "We got a little schooled that day by a leader who'd never been to business school, and likely hadn't even taken a business class. Here were all these executives with MBAs and tons of experience, and there she stands up and just says it like it is—right from her heart. People cheered like crazy when she reminded everyone at the company why we are all here," he recalls. Sturt continues:

> I remember my very first board meeting when I was promoted to the executive team. The board was talking about and reviewing the financial results of the company in a formal setting. We went through all the board discussion issues, capital expenditure plans, P&Ls, and so forth. When we got to the end of the meeting, I was really curious about what Carolyn would say. I was expecting her to ask about the dividend plan or some element of the financials. But instead she asked just two questions: (1) "How do our employees feel we're treating them?" and (2) "How do our customers feel about us and what we are doing for them?" I thought

to myself, "Wow!" Those kinds of questions from the chair of the board set a course for measuring yourself against things that are much bigger and more far reaching than the everyday operating metrics of a company.

A Foundation of Balance

Change is constant at O.C. Tanner, but its foundation remains stable. Because of this, the organization is nimble for its size and quick to adapt its strategy to an evolving marketplace.

The organization gives every employee annually a strategy map to highlight priorities and objectives for the coming year. There are elements on the map that have not changed in years and won't change in the foreseeable future—as they reflect the foundation of O.C. Tanner. Creating a level of stability that everyone can count on creates a sense of calm even in times of rapid change. It helps the organization move fast without destabilizing its workforce. This type of thinking is core to the DNA of who the O.C. Tanner Company is and how it effectively executes and grows its business year over year.

One example of its stability is captured by conduct during the Great Recession from December 2007 to June 2009. O.C. Tanner's CEO gathered all the employees together and explained that customers were going through tough times. For the first time in the company's history, customers were cutting back on spending, and O.C. Tanner had to respond accordingly. The organization saw an 8 percent drop in its revenue, and its strategy needed to reflect this reality. Despite this, the CEO insisted that the company not lose focus on its identity and its goals. He instructed the staff not to take their foot off the gas on continuing with the investments they needed to make in line with fulfilling O.C. Tanner's purpose and vision. The mandate was to continue full steam ahead but to look for ways to reduce nonessential expenses by 11 percent. He asked for everyone's help to avoid laying off a single person during the downturn.

The combination of a feeling of stability, a bedrock of values, and a consistency of purpose kept employees comforted, engaged, and loyal during times of pay freezes, reduced sales commissions, reorganizations, and doing without things that they had planned on. The organization's messaging as to why it existed, where it was going, and what it needed to do to get there continued as always.

When people start to hold themselves and others around them accountable for protecting your organization's culture, that's when you know it's truly institutionalized, not something orchestrated or pushed through a leadership team.

O.C. Tanner believes that focus equals power. A very clear, almost singular focus allows clarity and inspiration and draws people like a magnet. Purpose needs to be something that has a gravitational force to it. You know you have a purpose that is relevant and worth rallying around when people want to be part of it. It is not forced or contrived. It is something of worth: true, real, and authentic. Ensuring that you are executing on the right things effectively and consistently requires laser-sharp alignment with that purpose.

Accelerating Engagement

When I walked around the manufacturing site at O.C. Tanner, there was a clear buzz of engagement and dedication to what everyone was doing. Employees would stop what they were involved with to eagerly share their work and accomplishments with me. It was quite refreshing and different from many other manufacturing sites I had toured. Instead of employees keeping their heads down to avoid eye contact, these employees seemed to want to get my attention because they were proud of what they were making and wanted to show it off.

Managers on the manufacturing floor at O.C. Tanner have a daily huddle with their teams. This is quite common and something I have experienced at most manufacturing sites where I have worked or toured.

The difference with O.C. Tanner, though, is what the teams speak about. Of course, the goals and metrics that are displayed on boards and monitors by each team and expected for the day, week, and month are discussed. But the entire discussion is also tied to the bigger picture of O.C. Tanner—its purpose. During this huddle, colleagues are reminded not only of their goals for the day but why they are important to O.C. Tanner's overall purpose and its customers. They also get reminded about how each person's contribution helps fulfill the organization's purpose. Despite this practice being the ultimate igniter of meaningful work and people engagement, this alignment discussion rarely happens in organizations at any level. But great organizations get it.

At Stryker, patients who had their lives saved or improved as a result of the products the company produces are regularly brought into manufacturing sites or meetings to speak to employees. Knowing how work positively impacts the lives of others creates deep emotional meaning.

During my time at O.C. Tanner, I was told a story about an older production employee from Vietnam who polishes emblems at the company. While working, she was asked by her manager about her job. With a big smile she said, "I love what I do. This is going to make someone's day when they get this award." She went on to explain that she envisions the recognition award she is working on being delivered to someone at a company as she polishes it. The quality of her work matters to her because it has an important purpose. This purpose is directly tied to her execution and reinforced by every level of O.C. Tanner's organization. Thanks to this, people engagement, product quality, productivity, on-time delivery, customer satisfaction, sales, and profits are high.

Giving all the people in a business this line of sight to greater meaning is the ultimate accelerator of engagement and profits. Plus, the excitement, passion, and dedication that engaged people bring home every day and into the communities where they live make for a goodwill multiplier for your brand, product, and organization. Metrics don't inspire, but the knowledge of how achieving them positively impacts the lives of others does. O.C. Tanner gets this, and its efforts to create alignment for its people shows up positively in its business results.

The Right People

All interviews at O.C. Tanner include a deliberate discussion about what the company does and why they do it. The process is designed to ensure proper new hire alignment from day one. If candidates don't believe in what O.C. Tanner is trying to do for the world, they are not a fit and won't be hired. This is determined first and foremost.

Hiring managers look into the eyes of their candidates, listen to what they have to say, and pay special attention to their body language. Candidates are asked to give examples and share stories of things that are important to them in life. "We are looking for things that strike a chord deep within them. Qualities that give a sense of kinship and belonging . . . birds of a feather," Sturt explains. Only those candidates who truly believe in the cause and purpose and have the ability to do the job well are hired.

Sturt recalls an interview he had with a man who was both talented and experienced. He initially seemed like a star candidate, until Sturt and his team started digging in a bit more and discussing O.C. Tanner's purpose, vision, and mission. It became clear at that point that he was not a cultural fit. They passed on him. "If there is even a little question about their fit and cultural connection to what we're doing—in virtually every case we get six months, a year, or sometimes two years down the tracks, it stops working. Some of those individuals will try to change the culture and insert their own sense of direction. If it runs counter to the purpose of the organization, eventually, it just does not work and they have to leave," Sturt says.

O.C. Tanner's key to hiring success is looking for connections to the company's purpose and values, not trying to find people who think the same way as their hiring manager or others in the organization. To avoid groupthink, the organization deliberately looks for diverse thinkers who also align with their common purpose.

Walking the Talk

Operating and executing with a high level of purpose requires that your organization practices what it preaches—that it leads by example in all that it does. A personal story that Sturt shared with me captures this concept superbly.

In 1999, at the height of the Internet boom, Sturt had received an offer to join a start-up in Portland, Oregon, called Learning.com. The organization was starting from nothing to create some sort of Internet company for schools. Sturt decided to take all he had learned and apply it to heading up product development for this start-up.

Despite seven wonderful years at O.C. Tanner, Sturt had always wanted to try his hand at a start-up and knew this was his opportunity. His kids were still young, and he had the financial means to take the risk.

Sturt received some friendly ribbing and flak from his coworkers about chasing the "Internet dream," but everyone was extremely kind and supportive. Knowing he enjoyed Asian food, his team scheduled a lunch at a local Chinese restaurant to give Sturt a proper send-off and wish him well. As attendees were giving him some gag gifts and having a bit of fun, the CEO, Kent Murdock, and his COO came walking in. Sturt was not an executive at the time and therefore did not have a lot of interaction with either of them.

According to Sturt, Murdock approached the party and said he wanted to say a few words. "I really thought he was going to roast me. Saying, 'You know we've invested all of this money in you, brought in all of these consultants, given you all this education on the company's dime, and now you're leaving us for an Internet start-up? You scoundrel! Don't let the door hit you on the way out!'" Sturt shared.

Instead, Sturt says, Murdock told them, "I just wanted to come and personally express my appreciation to David for the work he's done." He went on to say kind things about the influence Sturt had on the company and some of the web-based products he'd helped create and the team he led.

Then, Murdock added that he wanted to let Sturt know that if, for any reason, the Internet bubble burst or if he just decided that he missed the company, he was welcome back at O.C. Tanner. Murdock then reached into his jacket pocket and pulled out a Delta one-way ticket from Portland to Salt Lake City and presented the ticket to Sturt, telling him that they'd be honored to have him back at any time.

Sturt admits to having chills down his neck whenever he remembers that experience. I had the same reaction. How apropos for a reward and recognition organization to behave in such a way? How unfortunately rare it is for an organization to live what it stands for in such an intense way?

Two and a half years later, Learning.com—after many struggles—had turned the corner and was growing fast. Bright days were finally on the horizon. Again, Sturt was surprised by a call from Murdock, who said O.C. Tanner had just parted ways with its executive VP of marketing, and Murdock had thought of him.

Sturt was finally experiencing some success with the new venture and didn't have plans to leave. Murdock asked him to mull it over, chat with his wife, and then talk again in a week. Sturt did, and after several additional calls, he decided to return to O.C. Tanner.

"I honestly never thought I'd come back," Sturt admits, but because of who Murdock is, what he did for him when he resigned, and what O.C. Tanner stands for and believes in, he felt compelled to. "I felt so valued and appreciated at O.C. Tanner and it stuck with me," Sturt says.

Sturt's story illustrates the power of living and executing on pure purpose in an organization. It attracts and retains the best talent, engages those within and around your organization, and consequently drives business outcomes.

Gap's Balance

This Way Ahead, the program launched by the retailer Gap to connect low-income youth to its entry-level jobs and career coaching, mentioned earlier in this book, is another strong example of a purpose feeding business execution and vice versa. Not only does the organization's program have social value connected to its purpose, but it is also closely tied into its business outcomes. The kids who come through this program end up staying with Gap twice as long, are more engaged, and produce better results. The company measures not only whether its programs are positively impacting lives but also how the programs positively impact its business. The organization's purpose meets its business execution to improve financial outcomes—reduced cost of turnover, better-quality work, higher customer satisfaction, increased sales, and enhanced profits.

Dan Henkle, president of Gap Foundation, says that the sustainability of any type of program Gap launches depends on two things. The program must (1) have social value—do good—and (2) be good for the business—produce positive business outcomes. "These are the programs that we will scale at Gap for a long time to come," Henkle explains. Clear metrics connected to these programs measure employee retention, absenteeism, productivity, self-esteem, and self-confidence, which all feed into Gap's business results.

All the work Gap has done around greenhouse gas emissions is another good example. "Not only is the focus good for our planet," Henkle says, "it spurred innovation and the way Gap thinks about its own energy management. Any time we become more energy efficient, it's of course better for the environment, but also produces tremendous results in terms of energy efficiency and cost savings for us."

Gap's balance of purpose and execution requires both internal and external coordination and partnerships. A big theme for Gap is integration. This means that every initiative has identified partners to ensure it gets implemented correctly and when expected. With Gap's energy efficiency, for example, all partners inside and outside the company are expected to look at energy procurement and management. It is part of the requirement for ongoing relationships.

Henkle explained that if Gap's one hundred thirty-five thousand employees all feel that part of their job is to be ambassadors for the work they are doing, then that attitude is going to propel that work. If the company has the same expectations for well-aligned external partners to move their cause forward, scaling its programs becomes much easier.

Like the focus of a good HR function, Henkle explains:

> If you have better and better leaders, they [the leaders] need less and less of your support. It's the same thing for everyone's accountability. If you can build in doing the right thing, it's less of a push from the center. It's how we get things done.

In this framework, the most sophisticated programs should have the leanest centralized groups and be the initiatives happening throughout the business every day as part of the organization's DNA.

Everything Gap does in line with its organizational purpose is in some way correlated to the company's bottom line. There is a balanced ROI of doing social good and delivering on needed business results. This formula has enabled Gap to grow at a rapid rate and remain financially profitable. Plus, the company is reinvesting in its business by hiring more purpose-minded people, opening more stores, acquiring more businesses, and fulfilling its organizational purpose in a sustainable manner. Henkle believes that more and more customers will be voting with their money in the future. Running a great business that adds both social and economic value is key to customer engagement and loyalty now and in the foreseeable future. This will only intensify as customers continue to push companies to do more, especially in light of the accelerating power of social media.

Walmart's Balance

Walmart founder Sam Walton's goal from day one was "great value and great customer service." Great value is created through great execution. Walton rallied his employees with "If we work together . . . we'll give the world an opportunity to see what it's like to save and have a better life."[4]

To support the selling of low-cost products to its customers, Walmart, by the dictates of its very purpose, must run a lean operation. If overhead was too high, the company would never be able to fulfill its purpose. Every penny counts to its customers and, subsequently, to its business.

Vendors are strictly managed to control cost and inventory. If vendors can't meet Walmart's strict and established supply chain management requirements, the relationship is quickly terminated. Walmart's purpose simply can't afford a misstep on execution.

If Walmart fails to execute at a high level, it will not be able to deliver its promise of helping customers save money. If its customers can't save money, they can't live better. If they don't live better, Walmart loses the very reason its customers are loyal to the store. They will start shopping elsewhere, sales will decline, profits will disappear, and an empire will crumble.

Walmart has been able to change the face of retail through its balance of purpose and execution. If Walmart promised low prices but ran a poor business with substandard execution, the promise would be nothing more than a saying on a wall. Customers would not believe in or trust the brand. They would ultimately be driven to competitors that offered better value. But thanks to its connection between purpose and execution, Walmart employs 1 percent of America and 2.2 million worldwide. The company is now worth a half trillion dollars and is growing.

Both Today and Tomorrow Matter

A CEO I worked with early in my career demanded that both short-term and long-term objectives be met. At the time, I challenged his thinking by believing that organizations had to take hits today to meet tomorrow's goals and aspirations—the organization's ultimate purpose. I have since learned that this philosophy can be a business killer. In fact, most investors care more about short-term results than they do about the future. This stems from a combination of humanity—propelled by innovation and technology—moving more rapidly than ever before with a basic desire for instant gratification. The world no longer engages generations of workers for a three-hundred-year-long building project.

As we established, purpose is an organization's *why*: why it was started in the first place. To make organizational purpose work, you must engage your people and customers around it over the short- and long-term. The results show that the better the alignment between personal and organizational purpose, the more business success you will achieve. To make execution work, you must deliver on business objectives in line with your organization's purpose. You may want to change the world, but if you can't deliver on organizational promises and business needs now and in the future, you won't.

To effectively balance purpose and execution, your short- and long-term organizational business strategy must make the two inseparable. The closer the alignment, the better business outcomes you will achieve.

Chapter Questions

To understand how well your organization is balancing its purpose and execution, ask yourself the following questions. If you can't answer yes to all of the following questions and those around you feel the same way, you will need to focus your efforts on rebalancing your organizational purpose and business execution.

- Does our focus on organizational purpose equal our focus on business execution?

- Do our organizational strategies feed a sustainable business model directed toward fulfilling our organizational purpose?
- Are we focusing on and delivering short- and long-term business results?

Notes

1. Southwest Airlines. "About." www.southwest.com/html/about-southwest/index.html?tab.
2. Yelp. "About." www.yelp.com/about.
3. Simon Sinek. *Start with Why: How Great Leaders Inspire Everyone to Take Action*. New York: Portfolio, December 27, 2011.
4. Walmart corporate website. "Our Story." http://corporate.walmart.com/our-story/our-history.

PART II

Creating One Team

CHAPTER 6

Establishing Trust

> *Trust is the glue of life. It's the most essential ingredient in effective communication. It's the foundational principle that holds all relationships.*
>
> —Stephen Covey

In Brent Gleeson's *Inc.* article "7 Simple Ways to Lead by Example," he states,

> Navy SEALs are trained to be leaders, regardless of age or rank. To put it another way, they are trained to earn trust. As I learned with the SEALs, and relearn continually in business, people truly follow only those they trust.[1]

I was lucky enough to work with several former Navy SEALs in my career. They reliably ranked among the top leaders in each organization. Building trust through leading by example is core to their belief system. The Navy SEAL Creed states, "I serve with honor on and off the battlefield . . . I lead by example in all situations."

All fruitful relationships in life require trust as their foundations. This is especially true when trying to build a healthy and thriving organizational culture—it is the bedrock of truly influential leadership. If you don't walk the talk, you will fail to drive or influence change.

Establishing and reinforcing trust requires actions that demonstrate care for people—in corporations and in personal life. Before you can expect any person in your organization to sign up for a cultural change initiative, they must trust you and your motives. If they feel that you and your organization truly believe in the concept of taking care of people to drive business results, the door is wide open to introduce Purpose Meets Execution. On the other hand, if your people believe that any new initiative is just window dressing to give the impression that the organization's people come first, all efforts will fail.

Demonstrating Care to Establish Trust

A CEO once told me his organization was not the "caring type." He was removed from his role not long after, as his business results continued to travel in the wrong direction.

Another CEO once partially agreed with my guidance that his organization needs to care for employees. "Yes, we need to care about our top performers," he replied. "Actually," I corrected, "we need to care about *all* our employees." I explained to him that the best leaders care for top performers by rewarding and recognizing them. And we care for lower performers by helping them improve their performance or by assisting them to move on to a place where they will be more successful. He listened, understood, and finally agreed.

Great leaders express concern for all their people, which creates a culture of trust. They sincerely care about their people's success, even beyond the job they are doing. It's a 360-degree outlook that encompasses people's jobs, careers, personal interests, health, happiness, families, and friends.

The *Harvard Business Review* article, "Employees Who Feel Love Perform Better," cites a study surveying 3,201 employees in seven different industries.[2] The study found that employees who felt they worked in a caring culture reported higher levels of job satisfaction and teamwork than those who did not. Plus, those workers recognized an increased commitment to their organizations and accountability for their performance.

The study demonstrates the correlation between caring for your people, trust, and organizational success. It concludes that caring for your people is good for them, your customers, and your business.

Managing with Care

Performance management is often overlooked while building a culture of trust, but it is undeniably one of the most important ways to show you care. My motto as an HR leader has always been, "Help people succeed in *life*." If someone is not performing in the job she is in, it does not mean that she is a bad person. It may simply mean she is in the wrong role, at the wrong organization, or working for the wrong manager. Poor performance is not necessarily a reflection of someone's abilities or talents; she just may require better alignment at work and in life. Help these people see their misalignment through coaching and through open and honest communication and feedback, and you will demonstrate sincere care and establish trust.

Living my motto has helped me save organizations hundreds of thousands of dollars in expenses connected to mismanagement of under-performers. In one case, these tactics turned an employee about to be unfairly terminated for performance into one who made a $1 million sale, once he'd received appropriate care and development. The particular employee had lagging sales and was frustrating his manager by what appeared to be a lack of interest in his job. It turned out that he simply wasn't getting the attention or direction he needed to succeed. When he was given a detailed Performance Improvement Plan (PIP), he finally got the support and clear direction he needed to win. He followed the plan with the assistance of an enlightened manager and turned his performance around in a big way.

Most people who file lawsuits or grievances against their employer do so because they feel they were treated unfairly and they were uncared for, overall. In most cases, the lawsuit comes in an effort to get even with a direct-line manager. These people may still love the organization and what it stands for, but the mistrust that stems from feeling uncared for overshadows any such feelings. This type of relationship also has a hugely negative impact on people engagement at every level of an organization.

There is a saying that people don't leave organizations, they leave managers. This is true because lack of trust is almost always at the core of a decision to leave. Managers, like most people, want to be liked. This is where the problem starts. To avoid potentially uncomfortable conversations, they duck honest discussions connected to poor performance. This leaves their people blind to performance that may not be meeting expectations. As a manager, realize that telling people when they are not meeting expectations can actually be a caring action that builds trust by helping them self-direct before it is too late. Or an honest and kind conversation can help an individual realize that the job or company is not for him. The person may choose to leave on his own to achieve success elsewhere—and this, too, is okay. Ironically, one of the most surefire ways to be disliked is not to discuss performance issues when they arise. If you have ever had to terminate an employee with nothing but great performance reviews, you will know what I mean.

It should also be noted that managers who fail to address poor performers demonstrate a lack of care for the entire team, who most likely want to perform at a high level. There is nothing that will drag down team engagement and performance and erode trust faster than allowing low performance to go unchecked. Even the highest-performing team members will start lowering the bar when they see others operating at a substandard level.

Overlooking the power of rewarding and recognizing exceptional work can also erode trust. People who don't feel their contributions are recognized lose trust in your culture and become disengaged.

Caring for a Whole Person

Caring for your people during working hours is only half the requirement. It is easy to fall into the trap of caring about or focusing on only the things people do for you while they are at work. But you know from personal experience that people's lives include more than their jobs. Leaders who don't respect this balance set up their business for mediocre results, at best. They also push their people toward resentment and regret later in life.

Caring for your people effectively is not difficult. In fact, it is the simple, easy, and free things that matter most. Remembering a birthday or asking about a person's weekend. Inquiring about a child's birthday party or catching up about the person's night school progress. Cheering on her marathon training or asking if she is feeling better after being out sick. All of these small actions show caring and go a long way.

Discuss life outside work, including things that are more important to your people than the work grind. Truly engaging a whole person accomplishes more than any amount of money or complex reward or recognition system could. Most people can't recall who handed them a cash bonus or certificate or even what it was for, but when an organization or boss showed care for them in a time of need or celebration, the memory will be fresh.

Anything you can do for your people to help them be successful in their roles and at your organization goes miles toward showing you care for them and builds a strong bond of trust. But helping your people succeed in life—in their job, career, and personal endeavors—matters the most to them and to your business.

A critical step toward continuous organizational improvement and attracting and retaining the best of the younger-generation workforce is the recognition that people's lives matter as a whole. Gen Y and gen Z get this mindset and demand it of their employers, too. In a little over a decade, nearly the entire workforce will embrace this mindset. Businesses that don't adapt to this way of thinking will not be able to compete for the best talent.

Organizations are not special, but the way they care about the success of their people is. Understanding and committing to the importance of creating a successful life for your people will maximize their engagement, retention, business results, and ultimately their ability to fully trust you and your organization.

Employing leaders and managers who are strong coaches and mentors and focus on both the short- and long-term career and personal objectives of their people is the best way to support and empower your people's success. The more you care for your people, the more they will trust you and the better business results you will achieve.

Assessing your organization's physical office space is also important. Closed-off executive, HR, legal, and finance departments or frequently closed office doors do not foster trust. I have experienced organizations where the legal department had restricted passcode access, the executives sat in a private enclosure, and the HR department was separated from the rest of the business. It felt like something sinister was going on.

Actions Speak Louder Than Words

Selling and marketing the principle of trust in your organization is certainly part of the initial equation if your culture lacks it, but actions always speak louder than words. In fact, a study of organizations that have high trust, discussed in *Strengths Based Leadership* by Tom Rath and Barry Conchie, yielded an insightful finding.[3] Companies that are perceived as having a high-trust culture spoke very little about trust, if at all. Trust is part of the DNA and leadership of the company. It exists simply because of the way people and leaders in the organization naturally behave every day. Leaders at these organizations even had a difficult time coming up with bullet points about what they actually do that resulted in the high-trust culture.

For more than thirty years, the Yonkers, New York–based Greyston Bakery has maintained a policy that encourages anyone to apply for employment, regardless of his education or criminal record. Profits from the organization support day care centers, health clinics, and counseling services. Its cakes have been served in the finest restaurants and at the White House. As Rebecca Leung reports in her article, "Greyston Bakery: Let 'Em Eat Cake," "The bakery doesn't hire people to make cakes. It makes cakes to hire people."[4]

Mike Brady, the bakery's CEO, is committed first and foremost to helping people succeed in life. Greyston's commitment to human growth and potential gives people a second chance at life, and the organization is winning because of it.[5] Sales at the bakery have grown by more than 50 percent in the past four years, and it competes successfully in the global supply chains of Ben & Jerry's and Whole Foods Market.

Greyston differentiates itself by caring for people. It gives anyone a chance for employment without concern for the person's background or experience. It is a groundbreaking model that has attracted and engaged good people who needed a break in life, as well as customers who appreciate and support the way the company cares for humanity. Based on the organization's actions, there is no denying that trust is at the foundation of everything it does and has led to its great success.

If people don't trust you, their boss, or the leadership in your organization to do the right thing and act with transparency and integrity, they will not respect you, and you will never get the most out of them. Low or topical people engagement does not drive a high-performance culture and effectively limits your business results.

A national Gallup Poll highlighted that "the chances of employees being engaged at work when they do not trust the company's leaders are just one in 12."[6] The poll also revealed that the chance of engagement jumps to better than one in two when the organization's leadership is trusted.

In Stephen Covey's *Leading at the Speed of Trust*, he explains how high trust increases speed and reduces cost in all relationships, interactions, and transactions.[7] He emphasizes the fact that organizations that don't earn trust simply don't have the ability to achieve accelerated growth and sustainability. In fact, studies by organizations such as Watson Wyatt show that organizations with high trust outperform low-trust ones by nearly 300 percent.

If you have leaders in your organization who don't naturally instill trust, you will never realize the full benefits of Purpose Meets Execution. The very essence of leading with purpose requires trust at its foundation. I highly recommend moving people who are not trusted by their team to non-people-management roles or asking them to leave your organization. Once trust is broken, it is incredibly difficult to repair and never fully regained.

Establishing Big Ass Trust

As I was looking around for the perfect example of how to build a strong culture of trust, I received an e-mail from an employee at Big Ass Solutions.[8] She had seen some of my articles and wanted to share a story with me about her unique company. I knew of the business because as I walked through the manufacturing site at Tesla Motors each day, Big Ass Fans spun slowly and quietly above my head. But other than the fact that the company made huge fans and had a name you simply can't miss, I knew nothing about the organization—until the fortuitous e-mail.

After reading the employee's story about all the great cultural things going on at Big Ass Solutions, I poked around the company's website a bit. As I had hoped, it was funny and engaging. But—and this is a big but (I couldn't help myself!)—the organization is also clearly very serious about innovation, quality, customer satisfaction, and, most importantly, its people.

If you laughed at the name, you won't smirk at the company's impressive results. Big Ass Solutions was established in 1999 and had a first-year revenue of $433,000. In 2016, sales were nearly $250 million, up from $225 million in 2015. Starting with just five employees, it now has more than eleven hundred. Despite some questionable impressions of its brand (some people have been offended by the name, as the company website humorously notes), Big Ass Solutions is a real success story driven by a culture of care and trust.

Chief Big Ass Carey Smith (his real title) works under the idea that "we have to make money to stay in business, but we are not in business solely to make money." Smith is known for treating his people well, caring for them, and ultimately building trusting relationships. He doesn't call his people "employees." He refers to them as members of the tribe. "Each of us is reliant on others to be successful. By treating employees this way, it is safe to say we come to work ready to give 100 percent," one tribe member told me. "In fact, I'd say our dedication to our people is the reason we've grown so fast," Smith confirms.

Smith's secret to building a culture of Big Ass Trust involves four key tenets.

1. People Versus Profits

"I've been asked several times whether Big Ass Solutions puts people or profits first. In my mind, these are not separate objectives—they are the same goal. In a world where it seems like everyone is trying to screw everyone else over to make a buck, I still believe the best business deals benefit everyone involved," Smith explains.

Big Ass Solutions' three main stakeholders are their people, customers, and suppliers, and the company makes sure everyone walks away from every deal feeling like a winner. "When customers are happy, they feel good about their purchase and spread the word about Big Ass Solutions. The easiest way to make our customers happy is to keep our employees and suppliers happy as well," Smith adds.

The organization lives by the principle that when its people are happy, customers are well taken care of. And when suppliers are happy, they go above and beyond to make sure their parts are top-quality, so their products are, too.

2. The Tribe Mentality

"We're not quite a family—it's impossible to be that close when you've grown to the size we have—but we are a tribe," Smith explains. Tribe members at Big Ass look out for one another and keep one another's best interests in mind. With such rapid growth, they have to. Growth at this rate requires a great deal of collaboration and trust. Everyone has to be rowing in the same direction to keep the momentum going.

At Big Ass, management encourages collaboration by pushing people out of their comfort zones. They bring a mix of people—from production employees all the way up to the executive team—to new-hire dinners. They assign seating at office events so that people meet others who work outside their department. When they structure departments and projects, they purposely create a little positive friction between groups to force people to learn to work together and align their goals and budgets.

"I loathe interoffice politics," Smith admits, " . . . but I think there is much, much less at Big Ass Solutions than anywhere else because we've developed an open, honest, friendly culture. It's hard to be mad at someone or want to throw someone under the bus if you've met their spouse and you've all had drinks. You're much more inclined to figure out how to work together."

"Bringing people together also helps boost transparency since each employee has a better understanding of their counterparts' roles," a tribe member told me.

3. Failing Fast and Admitting Mistakes

"The biggest part of growing trust is being honest, and that means you have to admit your mistakes. It's harder than it sounds to find employees who buy into this culture. People are conditioned to succeed from an early age—they don't want to be acknowledged for making mistakes. But I say fail, and fail fast. Most importantly, own up to it and learn from it. Everyone makes mistakes, but obviously we don't want to make the same mistake over and over," Smith says.

Smith admits that it is a struggle to build this type of culture. You have to start at the top. You can't pretend you're a flawless leader whom nobody can ever question. "I've made lots of mistakes, and I'll admit them to anyone who wants to listen. I put a decade into growing my first business, but it never grew past about $1.4 million in annual revenue. It was a long, slow failure, which is why I say fail fast," Smith adds.

If your people are paralyzed by the fear of imperfection, they're going to live in a cocoon and never accomplish anything great. Plus, your organization is never going to innovate. Big Ass Solutions has found that the people who really embrace this key cultural tenet go far in the company.

4. Employee Pay and Perks

To ensure people at Big Ass Solutions do not have to stress about their personal finances, the company pays their people 20 to 40 percent more than state and national averages. "Truthfully, we don't just do it because it's the nice thing to do. It's an investment. Happier, more financially secure employees do better work," Smith concludes.

Their Stock Appreciation Rights (SARS) program rewards people at all levels of the organization for their contribution to the company's overall growth and their loyalty and dedication. The program is designed to build wealth, and, thanks to it, a few people working at Big Ass could actually be considered millionaires.

The organization subsidizes lunches, an on-site nurse, and free fresh fruit—600 to 700 pounds each week. Big Ass Solutions is also big on company events and has two full-time events and engagement coordinators whose entire job description is to make the lives of their people better.

Smith envisions a company that will last long past his time as Chief Big Ass. His desire and focus is "to build a community where our children and our children's children want to work. Every decision made today considers this long-term goal," a tribe member told me.

"No other company has a culture like ours—we have a way of living that just happens to be a business. It's relaxed and informal, but simultaneously serious. It is the definition of work hard, play hard. We didn't do it on purpose, we're just a bunch of smart asses, and it shows. It's a result of the people we bring in—smart, funny, curious, and hard-working," Smith shares.

The culture of care and trust that Big Ass Solutions has been able to build and its ability to effectively balance its purpose and execution have led to its tremendous business success and growth. Plus, it boasts an impressive 85 percent tribe member retention rate.

Akash Hira, the lighting project coordinator at Big Ass, summed up the company for me:

> Working here can be a little chaotic at times, but everybody has fun and we all share the same goal of providing energy-efficient comfort to the world. Plus, all of our processes are transparent—we have an open office environment so everyone knows what everyone else is working on and how it affects everyone else involved. Because we work so closely together, it helps that we're all smart and funny, and we enjoy each other's company. You have to have sense of humor to work at a company called Big Ass Solutions.

Chapter Questions

Assessing trust in an organization is not always easy. If trust does not exist in your business, asking questions of your people may not get you an honest answer. Instead, ask questions at the leadership level to pick up on cultural clues.

As I mentioned, organizations with high-trust cultures have them simply because of the natural way people behave every day. This stems from ensuring that people in your business share your values and always take caring actions that foster trust.

To determine the level of trust in your organization, discuss the following questions at the leadership level in your company. Starting at the C-suite is advisable. It does not hurt to ask frontline people in your business, too, but again, be cautious of their responses if you sense your organization has a trust challenge.

- Do people openly and freely share information at my organization?
- Is there an effective and regularly used performance management and reward and recognition system at my organization?
- Do people regularly offer suggestions to improve challenges and take advantage of opportunities at my organization?
- Are office doors mostly open at my organization?
- Is senior leadership seen and accessible at my organization?

Notes

1. Brent Gleeson. "7 Simple Ways to Lead by Example." *Inc.*, April 23, 2013. www.inc.com/brent-gleeson/7-ways-to-lead-by-example.html.
2. Sigal Barsade and Olivia A. O'Neill. "Employees Who Feel Love Perform Better." *Harvard Business Review*, January 13, 2014. https://hbr.org/2014/01/employees-who-feel-love-perform-better.
3. Tom Rath and Barry Conchie. *Strengths Based Leadership*. New York: Gallup Press. September 1, 2013.
4. Rebecca Leung. "Greyston Bakery: Let 'Em Eat Cake." *CBS News*, June 27, 2004. www.cbsnews.com/news/greyston-bakery-let-em-eat-cake-27-07-2004/.
5. Greyston Bakery. "The Bakery That Gave Him a Second Chance." *Upworthy*. www.youtube.com/watch?v=pyI7pwbtNBo&feature=youtu.be.
6. Rath and Conchie. *Strengths Based Leadership*, p. 83.
7. Stephen Covey. "Leading at the Speed of Trust." www.youtube.com/watch?v=igyxxYShXYo.
8. Big Ass Solutions. www.bigassfans.com/company/.

CHAPTER 7

Accelerating People Engagement

> *When people are financially invested, they want a return. When people are emotionally invested, they want to contribute.*
>
> —Simon Sinek

Accelerating people engagement at your organization matters to your business. Gallup reports that companies with highly engaged workforces outperform their peers by 147 percent in earnings per share.[1]

The principle of maintaining a high-engagement and high-performance culture is simple: get people who love to do what you need them to do, place them in roles where they are playing to what they do best, and give them all the support and development they need to win. Then get out of their way.

It works like this. People whose careers empower them to feel aligned with what they believe they have been put on Earth to do care more than those who aren't. These people feel a great sense of meaning, commitment, and pride in their work. This alignment is connected to the heart of what they do and who they are. This creates an honest love for their life's endeavors. They don't see their activities as work but as part of their lives. They would perform such duties without pay and frequently do on their own time or while trying to find paying work (e.g., child care, art, writing, photography, charity work, car repair, neighborhood watch, political campaign work or lobbying, coaching, pro bono law, accounting, or pet rescue). Perfect alignment occurs when someone gets paid to do what he loves. The money—while a necessity for most—may be seen as a bonus instead of a motivator when people are truly aligned. This is where the magic of accelerated people engagement happens.

Playing to strengths is where executional excellence comes into play. No matter how much a person may love something, if she doesn't do it well, she will never set records, win medals, or be a high performer doing it.

I have loved running since high school. At my peak, I run twenty-five to thirty miles a week. I have fairly decent endurance and moderate speed. However, even if I ran every day of my life, had the best shoes and equipment, Olympic trainers, and no distractions, I could never run a marathon even remotely close to 2:02:57, the fastest in recorded history. While I love running, it is not a strength of mine. That is not to say that the miles I put in each week and the half marathons I have completed in less than two hours don't get me praise—they do. But there are many, many runners on this planet who are far better than me. I am okay—perhaps good but not great.

To deliver world-class performance, win gold medals, and exceed expectations on performance reviews (in organizations that set the bar correctly), you must be *great* at what you do.

The easiest way to assess whether people are in the right role is simply to ask them and those around them. As when you were assessing leadership, ask:

- What do you believe you do best?
- What do you do in life where you get the most positive feedback?
- What do you do in life where you get the most negative feedback?
- *To those who work with the person you are assessing, ask the following:* What do you believe this person does best? When do his talents shine?

The insights you gain from the answers to these questions will give you an accurate assessment of the strengths of the people in your organization and how well they will execute in their jobs. Their correct placement makes the difference between poor, good, and great performance.

Once you have ensured that you have the right people in the right roles, you need to give them the tools, resources, support, and development they need to win. Returning to my running example, even if I did have a world record in me, I could never achieve it without the best shoes, trainers, and focus. Giving well-placed people the things they need to run fast produces accelerated engagement and results. Finally, when everything is in place, just get out of the person's way.

When I worked at Stryker, I had the pleasure of interacting with John Brown, the celebrated CEO. About fifteen years ago, he shared a story with me that has stayed with me ever since. When he was young, he worked with his father on their farm. One day while helping his father, he got in the way of some work being done and was knocked to the ground. His father responded by instructing young Brown that when people are working, you need to get out of their way. Brown said that he never forgot his father's lesson. When people are working, get out of their way and let them do what you hired them to do.

World-Class Engagement

A friend of mine owns a local martial arts school in Arizona. His passion for the art form and his business are contagious. As he grows his business, his primary concern is maintaining the quality brand he worked so hard to build. Despite having several employees, he still personally wipes down all his studio mats because, "No one else cleans them as well as me," he told me. "No one cares as much."

My friend's challenge is exactly the same as the one that CEOs of Fortune 500 companies face, too: how do you get your people to care as much as you?

This is the challenge of achieving a culture that nurtures the highest level of engagement at all layers of your organization. Three buckets of engagement are important to know and recognize when assessing and segmenting your workforce. They are:

- **Actively disengaged.** These are people who are destructive in your business and actively work against your organizational purpose and what you are trying to accomplish. They go out of their way to generate negative results. They may intentionally destroy company property, undermine leadership direction, spread false rumors, be insubordinate, or purposefully be negative to upset others. These people need to be immediately managed into an "engaged" bucket or to leave your business as quickly as possible—in a respectful and caring way, of course.
- **Not engaged.** These people are those who have a nine-to-five mentality, but not necessarily those who simply have a nine-to-five schedule. These people mentally clock in and out and do nothing extra. While every organization will have some of these types of people—especially bigger companies—high-performing organizations do not exist with a majority of such people. Again, these people need to be moved up into the engaged bucket or hopefully replaced with an engaged person in the future. They may not be damaging to your business or as urgent to engage as people in the actively disengaged bucket, but they are not going to help take your organization to the next level either. I like to use the 80/20 rule as a good bar for where people should land. Essentially, 80 percent of your people should be in the engaged bucket.
- **Engaged.** These people are emotionally committed, they love what they do, and they go the extra mile every time. In a perfect world, every person you have in your business would jump out of bed each morning excited to contribute to your company's mission and purpose. Just imagine what that would look like in your organization. Imagine the additional productivity, quality, and care of work that would be delivered to your customers.

Under Purpose Meets Execution, four mindsets speak to the heart of accelerating people engagement and moving people into an engaged bucket. They all address creating owners versus "employees" in your business, regardless of the existence of financial ownership programs. Studies have shown that the war for the best next-generation talent includes an attraction based on this entrepreneurial element.

1. No Small Roles

Seventeen years later, I can still remember Nancy. She was friendly, talkative, knowledgeable, and engaging—a delightful person. She made me feel special and at ease as I waited in the lobby for my first interview at Stryker. After interacting with her, I wanted to work for the organization even more. Nancy was a receptionist. For me, she was the face of the multibillion-dollar organization.

Nancy was genuine in every way, but she also believed that her role was one of the most important at the organization. As I got to know her, I learned that her goal was to ensure that everyone she spoke to and met wanted to work for or do business with Stryker. She was a receptionist on par with the CEO and cared as much as he did about the success of the organization. She had a big and important role at Stryker.

The most amazing twist, which I witnessed in the division where I started working, was that almost everyone else also felt like Nancy. All the people working there saw their roles as critical to the success of the organization. Whether they were hand-finishing a knee-replacement product, packaging it, quality checking it, designing it, marketing it, selling it, or leading the people who did these tasks, all the employees felt they had a big and important role.

People engagement was high because, no matter what role you performed at the company, management at all levels made sure people knew how important they and what they were doing were to Stryker. Despite the division president overseeing close to three thousand people, he knew the name of almost every person, and he greeted people in the hallways like they were the only person working at the organization. He made people feel important, so no one wanted to let him, the organization, or our customers down. Plus, because people knew how their day-to-day actions fed into helping medical professionals improve and save the lives of their patients, they felt a personal responsibility to this important purpose.

The famous Russian director Constantin Stanislavski once said, "Theatre begins at the cloakroom."[2] By this, Stanislavski meant that his audiences must experience the magic of his productions the moment they stepped into the theater—from the ticket taker to the ushers who showed them their seats, everyone involved was helping create a magical experience for theatergoers. Stanislavski engaged everyone he worked with to bring his art to life. Whether you were working the front door or theater bar or starring in the production on stage, everyone was a part owner in the final product. This is what true purpose-focused leaders do. They accelerate people engagement by connecting the dots for everyone involved in shared endeavors.

As a trained theatrical director myself, I don't believe that there are small roles, only small actors. Ensure that all your people know the important role they play in your organization. People engagement will quickly rise, and business results will follow.

2. Leadership with Purpose

When my wife and I toured the maternity ward of Scottsdale Healthcare in anticipation of the birth of our second daughter, we encountered a powerful purpose-driven people engagement practice.

After about ten minutes of being led through the hospital hallways, we heard the sound of a lullaby filling the air from ceiling speakers. Our volunteer guide stopped and smiled, as did almost everyone else in the area.

In a soft voice, our tour guide said, "Do you hear that? That is the sound of another one of our babies being born. Every time a child is born here, that lullaby plays throughout the ward to announce the new arrival. Everyone always stops and smiles when this happens."

It seems almost impossible for anyone working in a maternity ward to forget why he is there. Being surrounded by newborn babies and moms on a daily basis would surely serve as the best reminder. However, in the day-to-day grind of any job at any company, people can lose focus on the reason for the organization's very existence. While playing a lullaby in the halls is clearly not an appropriate solution for most businesses, there are other simple ways of accomplishing the same objective. A software company where I worked notified the whole organization whenever a new customer deal was closed; a business I worked with in South Africa would ring a bell; the Safeway supermarket where I shop is "committed to improving the quality of life in the communities we [they] serve"[3] and, during a charity drive, announced donations that employees collected throughout the store for a chosen cause. A bank I worked with shares client videos, too. And, from 1955 to 1994, McDonald's proudly displayed on its restaurant signs the number of hamburgers it had served.[4,5] The practice stopped after 99 billion.

Keeping the reason your organization exists—its purpose—in front of your people's eyes and ears at all times helps keep everyone focused on the end game and accelerates people engagement and business outcomes in that direction. This is the responsibility of every manager and leader in a business.

3. Okay to Learn from Mistakes

Since high school, I have been a bit of serial entrepreneur, starting and owning businesses ranging from local advertising, to ear piercing product distribution, to live theater production, and now to my consulting practice. Despite the variety of my business endeavors, the one constant I found in business ownership is the need to experiment, fail, learn from mistakes, and try again. It is part of the journey to business success.

Working in a culture where people are afraid to make mistakes is stressful. This limits the possibilities of discovering new and better ways of doing things and reinforces the "just a job" mentality, rather than promoting ownership. True "ownership" comes from a sense of empowerment to experiment and fail. This applies to every organization, from not-for-profits to Fortune 500 companies, and to every position, from CEOs to receptionists. Unless you are working in a job where errors can cost a life or cause serious injury, there should be no harm in making them—as long as you learn from them.

The award-winning global design firm IDEO illustrates how empowering employees to act as owners in the pursuit of innovation can pay big dividends. The organization's slogan is "Fail often to succeed sooner," which supports its company-wide focus on "failing forward." The firm's human-centered philosophy has led to innovations ranging from the first computer mouse for Apple, to the robotic whale in the movie *Free Willy*, to hundreds of name-brand products most of us use every day, including the first stand-up toothpaste tube. In addition to yielding a strong sense of ownership, IDEO's culture has led to high people engagement, low turnover, and strong business outcomes.

4. One Team

I have worked with many senior leaders who try to break down silos and barrier walls in their organizations to create one team. In most cases, I have found that structures that incent and celebrate individual and department contributions over organizationally driven goals are to blame. Plus, physical structures like closed office plans and executive office areas create additional obstacles to embracing a one-team mindset.

In organizations that live with silos, competition is often wrongly focused more internally than externally against true competitors. Plus, resources are wasted and duplicated, and the ability to move fast is dampened. When physical office barriers exist, hidden agendas, people separation, low trust, and disengagement tend to permeate.

If infrastructure elements like leader bonuses based solely on their function or business area are in place, the likelihood of silos forming is high. The same applies to reporting lines that remain completely compartmentalized. When trying to build a one-team culture, at least a valuable percentage of incentive pay must be tied to collaboration and the bigger organizational picture. Plus, reporting lines that build bridges to other interdependent departments or businesses are helpful, even if they're only dotted lines.

Flat and open organizational structures and environments foster a one-team culture, promote transparency and collaboration, and accelerate people engagement.

At W.L. Gore & Associates headquarters in Newark, Delaware—the company famous for Gore-Tex—there are associates but no employees, sponsors but no bosses, and specific work areas but no traditional organizational charts. Leaders emerge based on what Gore calls "followership"—the people of the organization decide who is qualified to be a leader based on the willingness of others to follow them. The lack of hierarchy and "bosses" fosters autonomy and a sense of ownership for all people working at the company. The organization's high level of people engagement has put it on Fortune's 100 Best Companies to Work for in America for nineteen consecutive years.

Overall, the more people feel like owners in your business, the greater the engagement in your organization and the better your business results. In recognition of this idea, LinkedIn's core values include a phrase that states, "Act like an owner." The statement is more than words to the company. LinkedIn built its culture around this tenet, which mirrors the life of an entrepreneur: unlimited vacation in line with business needs, "inDays" one Friday a month where employees can work on personal projects, $5,000 a year for professional education, a platform called Incubator that allows employees to pitch ideas to executives, an opportunity to compete for up to a $10,000 donation to the charity of the employee's choice or to start one's own charity, and personal grants that allow employees to become involved in independent charity work.

If you are ever lucky enough to have a meal at LinkedIn's Mountain View, California, headquarters, it is quite a treat. The on-site café emulates an expensive Las Vegas buffet. Here, employees take what they want and eat for free. They don't even need to check out with someone before heading to their table. But it gets better. The company also allows family and friends to visit employees for meals and eat for free, too. I was told that on Friday mornings, employees have their parents, grandparents, children, and friends eating breakfast with them. LinkedIn does not track who eats the meals. It trusts its people to enjoy the benefit as part of work–life *integration*, not balance.

We All Understand Engagement

Anyone who has ever been in a retail store understands the importance of people engagement in a business. Have you ever been in a store where the person you interact with hates her job, company, and life? What happens? You may buy less or leave the store with nothing at all. You will tell all your friends and family not to shop there. And you will most likely not shop there again yourself, if you can help it. This simple interaction with, most likely, a low-paid frontline person has a direct and immediate impact on top- and bottom-line business results.

What happens, in contrast, when you have the opposite experience? Imagine an interaction with a person in the right role who loves what she does and truly cares for her customers and organization. When you get to interact with someone like that, you may buy more than you were planning to because the salesperson inspires you and lifts your spirits. You will tell family and friends about your great experience and encourage them to shop at the business. You will return. Assuming a profitable business model, the business's top- and bottom-line results will improve.

The same principle applies to both external and internal customers. Even though internal business customers are more of a captive audience, poor interactions with internal departments in your organization will lead to a cycle of disengagement between those who deliver support and those who need it. If interacting with such people and departments can be avoided, people will. If interactions can't be avoided, they will be minimal and entered reluctantly. In all cases, these interactions will be less than productive, produce lower-quality work, and breed negativity in your business.

The best example of this customer experience ROI for me came when I recently purchased my first Harley-Davidson motorcycle. I had been riding and enjoying Honda motorcycles for about twenty-three years and still have no complaints with them. Whenever I had an issue—which was extremely rare—I would call a dealer, and my problem would be taken care of promptly. Despite my good experiences with Honda, my dream bike had always been a Harley cruiser. I had felt drawn to the brand ever since I was child. However, the price point between the two bikes kept me loyal to Honda early in my career. Within days of purchasing my 2016 Harley Davidson Softail Slim, I experienced the brand difference and how people engagement played a central role in it.

Removing the fuel cap on my past Hondas required one twist and a lift. When I went to fuel up my Harley for the first time, a twist did not allow me to remove the gas cap. Not wanting to force it and break my new, expensive dream bike, I called my dealership for assistance in getting the cap off. After an unsuccessful attempt to help me over the phone, the gentleman I was speaking with asked me where I was. I told him that I was about ten miles from the dealership near my home. Despite it being eight in the evening, he said he would send someone over to help me. As it was late and I was only about two miles from my home with plenty of gasoline to get me there, I told the man that it could wait until the next day. He said that he would be happy to send someone to my home in the morning to help.

The next morning, Jávier showed up at my door with a handlebar mustache, Harley shirt, and big smile. He walked into my garage and turned the gas cap on my bike, then he turned it again a bit harder. It came right off. Needless to say, I felt incredibly embarrassed. Had I turned the cap a second time and a bit harder, it would have come off for me, too. The cap required two twists instead of the one I was used to with my old bikes.

Despite my embarrassment, Jávier made me feel like I had done him a favor by having him come out to help me. He told me that it was not a problem at all and that Harleys work a little differently from other bikes. "Lots of new Harley riders have the same questions," he assured me. He then went the extra mile. "If you ever have any additional problems with your bike, here is my cell number. You can call me anytime, even at three in the morning, and I will help you out," he offered. It was an amazing gesture of customer service and engagement. Jávier is clearly a rider himself, loves what he does, and takes pride in helping his customers. He is engaged in what he does.

What Jávier and Harley did for me that day created a customer for life. Despite my good experiences with Honda, I could have never imagined customer service at this level. Jávier truly made me feel important, cared for, and valued. The salespeople at my dealership did the same. In fact, when I picked up my bike with my wife and youngest daughter (Curly, my baldheaded salesperson, called ahead to ensure I was bringing them with me), the whole store gathered around to watch me strike a large gong to commemorate the special occasion. This was followed by hugs and handshakes to welcome me into the Harley family. It was a remarkable experience all the way around. In my excitement, I bought a couple thousand dollars of accessories but left feeling good about the experience. I didn't even feel guilty about the extra money I had not really planned to spend. Subsequently, I have referred everyone I know looking for a bike to the Harley dealership where I bought mine.

Jávier's alignment to Harley's purpose, his clear talent and knack for his job, and his high level of engagement had both short- and long-term positive impacts on his organization's business results.

When I called Jávier to ask him for a picture of himself so I could share his story at a presentation, he was not on shift. Even though he was out with some friends, he said he would go home, put his Harley shirt on, and ask one of them to take a picture to send to me. In less than an hour, I had Jávier's smiling face in my presentation. He is remarkable, and I am so grateful for the story he has allowed me to share with others.

My personal illustration of this connection between engaged people working for a company and customer engagement and business results is one small source of evidence. The Gallup organization has done more than thirty years of research that has proven this direct correlation, too.[6]

The research shows that engaged teams are/experience:

15 percent more profitable,
30 percent more productive,
12 percent higher customer engagement,
30 percent less turnover,
62 percent less safety issues,
37 percent less absenteeism,
28 percent less shrinkage.

These percentages make sense. Engaged people will:

- be more cost conscientious,
- work harder to produce more and better products,
- make customers happier and more loyal,
- leave the organization less often,
- pay closer attention to the work they are doing and look out for others when it comes to safety,
- take fewer sick days,
- be less likely to steal from the organization.

All these improvements translate into more sales and a higher profit margin.

Plus, engaged people and cultures attract and keep the best talent. The best people will want to work at financially successful organizations where people are happy, safe, and respected for what they do. High people and customer engagement is critical to a strong employment brand and accelerated talent attraction. Most people want to work for an organization that others have good things to say about, whether in personal conversations or on web platforms like Glassdoor. Your word of mouth matters, especially when you need to hire a lot of people to meet growth targets. Plus, the expense of losing good talent adds up quickly in recruiting costs, retraining, and internal and external customer disruption.

Engagement Givens

As you accelerate people engagement through the lens of Purpose Meets Execution, there are some basic rules to understand.

- Purpose Meets Execution must start at the top. That means there must be full alignment and buy-in at the CEO and C-suite levels before the initiative cascades down in the organization. It is important to note that you can never fix lower levels of an organization if the top part is broken. Purpose Meets Execution must start at the top. The best people engagement initiatives are the ones where the CEO stands up and says, "This is what we are doing, this is why, and here's why it's crucial to you and our organization."
- All feedback obtained through Purpose Meets Execution should be reviewed and considered, regardless of any bias toward the information. I was once told after a presentation I gave that an organization recently dropped $12 million on a consultant to tell management what they would have known for free if they had just asked and listened to their people. Listening to your people costs nothing. Plus, what they have to say holds the keys to fixing any challenge or problem your organization may be facing. A hand finisher once told me that his manufacturing site would close in the near future, understanding the reality even before senior-level leaders knew it. He had worked at the site for thirty years, and his perspective from the front lines watching the product flow gave him an insight others did not have. Your people are intuitive. Their close proximity to your work product and its processes gives them

unique perspectives on what is right and wrong for your business. Listen to them.

- The Purpose Meets Execution platform, though focused on people engagement, is not an HR initiative, it's a business initiative. HR will need to take a critical role in supporting the initiative, but it must be led by functional business leaders at the C-suite level.
- As already discussed, a culture of care is essential to the success of Purpose Meets Execution and the acceleration of people engagement. Plus, caring for people is always the right thing to do.
- Decades of research have proven that the more you engage and care for your people (in all industries, big and small, globally), the better business results you will experience.
- An engaged culture matters over the short- and long-term for retention and attraction of the best talent.
- Knowing and focusing on your organization's *why*, *where*, and *what* are foundational to Purpose Meets Execution and to accelerated engagement. Plus, this emphasis helps ensure a consistency of organizational focus and culture in growing companies—both organically and through merger and acquisition.
- Even though Purpose Meets Execution survey feedback should be collected via an anonymous third-party platform, creating and maintaining a culture of high trust will ensure you get open and honest feedback when you ask for it. If people fear those in power in your organization, you will not get the information you need to improve your business. Encourage everyone to share the good, the bad, and the ugly. And commit to your people that action will be taken to improve the organization as a result of the feedback. If you don't know what the challenges and opportunities are, you can't do anything about them. It is also advisable to mention the Purpose Meets Execution Action Planning process that will be discussed in the next chapter.
- Purpose Meets Execution is not just an information-gathering exercise through a survey, interviews, and discussions. It is also a

business strategy to accelerate people engagement and drive business outcomes. The survey, interview, and discussion portion is just the tip of the iceberg that is needed to understand and diagnose what is going on. Everything that happens thereafter—the action each team and your organization take to overcome challenges and take advantage of opportunities—is what is most important.

Plus, if you ask your people for feedback and then do nothing about it, you should have never asked in the first place. Such complacency fosters disengagement and mistrust. If you ask for feedback and people see you have made changes as a result of it, more people will get on board, participation will rise, and engagement momentum will build. If you ask for feedback and do nothing about it, people will not waste their time giving it to you the next time you ask. Purpose Meets Execution's cycle involves gathering information, analyzing it, doing something about it, and then measuring again to assess improvements in engagement and business results.

- While giving Purpose Meets Execution feedback should never be mandatory, participation in the process is one of the strongest initial indicators of organizational engagement. If your people don't care enough or don't trust in the culture enough to take five or ten minutes out of their day to give helpful feedback, you have a people engagement challenge out of the gate. I never consider participation rates below 80 percent great. This is because those who did not offer feedback could have drastically changed the overall results if they had.

  For this reason, celebrating good overall results with low participation is not advisable. In most cases, it is the unhappy and disengaged people who abstain from participating in the feedback portion of Purpose Meets Execution. At organizations like Stryker, 98 percent employee participation rates on people engagement surveys are quite common. If you build the idea of people engagement into your cultural DNA, as Stryker has, your organization can achieve the same. People at Stryker believe in the process and see the results of their participation. Momentum is built into the system.

- Good communication before, during, and after the Purpose Meets Execution feedback stage is essential to gaining buy-in and building trust around the initiative. Telling people what is happening, why, and when provides clarity. Keeping people in the loop as feedback comes in establishes trust. Sharing what you learned fosters transparency. Celebrating what you did as a result of the feedback builds engagement momentum. Unless you are working in a utopian culture where everyone feels safe sharing feedback, overcommunicate and sell the fact that the Purpose Meets Execution online survey is anonymous. Also, assure your people that no one in the organization will see individual feedback and no team reports will be generated for teams with fewer than five participating members for autonomy reasons. Smaller teams will use their manager's report card for team Action Planning discussions.

Purpose Meets Execution Feedback Tool

Just as a doctor can't treat a sick patient without assessing symptoms, a business leader can't strengthen a corporate culture without diagnosing the challenges. The Purpose Meets Execution diagnostic tool has been created to measure the levels and balance of purpose and execution in all organizations, regardless of size or industry. The platform is designed to be simple and straightforward and is ultimately tied to a business ROI dashboard.

Purpose Meets Execution uses a six-point rating scale: strongly disagree, somewhat disagree, slightly disagree, slightly agree, somewhat agree, strongly agree.

The following Purpose Meets Execution statements should be asked and rated by all those working in your business through an anonymous third-party web platform. This will give your people peace of mind that their direct responses won't be seen by their manager, HR, or anyone else in the organization. More information on deploying Purpose Meets Execution can be found at PurposeMeetsExecution.com. You can also use applications such as SurveyMonkey or other online survey platforms. However, it is important that you are able to generate team Purpose Meets Execution reports and segment the feedback for analysis purposes. Being able to track action plans is also an important feature.

The first six Purpose Meets Execution statements pertain to organizational purpose. Statements 7 through 11 relate to executional excellence.

1. Anyone involved with my organization can explain why it is needed.
2. Those around me—including our customers—would agree on why this organization is needed.
3. The future vision of my organization is clearly communicated to those around me—including our customers.
4. Those around me—including our customers—care about the success of this organization.
5. Managers take an active interest in the lives of the people that work for them.
6. People believe that being part of this organization makes them a better person.
7. We always follow through on our promises at my organization.
8. The people at my organization are praised for the work they do.
9. My organization fulfills our customer's needs.
10. People's ideas are valued at my organization.
11. People believe the work they do at my organization makes a difference to its success.

The following two open-ended questions are included in the survey.

- What needs to change to make this organization more successful?
- Why does this organization matter to you and others?

In conjunction with the Purpose Meets Execution survey platform, one-on-one and team feedback sessions are also recommended to dig further into the information you receive from the survey or to ask questions that you believe may be helpful to your organization that are not captured on the Purpose Meets Execution survey.

Chapter Questions

As you read in this chapter, there are four key mindsets to accelerating people engagement at an organization. Ask and answer the following questions to determine where your organization excels—and where you may still need work. Discuss these questions with others inside your organization to get a deeper perspective.

No Small Roles:

- Are certain roles at my organization seen as more important than others?

Leadership with Purpose:

- Do I and others see and hear reminders of the organization's purpose each day?
- Do people in my organization see and hear regular reminders about how their daily work connects to the organization's purpose?

Okay to Learn from Mistakes:

- Do people in my organization feel comfortable making mistakes that they can learn from?
- Would anyone characterize my organization as having a culture of fear?

One Team:

- What percentage of time does my organization spend competing internally versus externally?

- Do people regularly use the words "I" or "we" when referring to work they do at my organization?
- *The use of "we" over "I" by your people has a direct correlation between how much "ownership" people feel in your organization.*

Notes

1. Susan Sorenson. "How Employee Engagement Drives Growth." *Gallup Business Journal*, June 20, 2013. www.gallup.com/businessjournal/163130/employee-engagement-drives-growth.aspx.
2. "Constantin Stanislavski." *Wikipedia*. http://en.wikipedia.org/wiki/Constantin_Stanislavski.
3. "Why Work for Us." *Safeway*. www.careersatsafeway.com/why-work-for-us.
4. Spencer Jakab. "McDonald's 300-Billionth Burger Delayed." *Wall Street Journal*, January 22, 2013. www.wsj.com/articles/SB10001424127887323301104578258113829116672.
5. "Our History." *McDonald's*. www.mcdonalds.com/us/en-us/about-us/our-history.html.
6. *Gallup, Inc*. "The Engaged Workplace." *Gallup Employee Engagement*, 2016. www.gallup.com/services/190118/engaged-workplace.aspx.

CHAPTER 8

Connecting People's Actions to the Bigger Picture

People have to understand what my game is. It's not all about numbers. There's a bigger picture here. I don't create off the dribble. I rely on my teammates; my role is to set screens and get rebounds.

—Rebecca Lobo, basketball player

I once had a CFO tell me that he felt spending just two hours a year with every team in the organization to discuss people engagement was a productivity issue. He just didn't see the value in it, and, in fact, he believed it was a waste of time. He clearly did not get it. When his organization's financials started to go the wrong way, wiser leadership relieved him of his role.

One of the most damaging things you can do to a culture is to ask people for feedback and then do nothing about it. Doing this erodes trust and makes people feel they have wasted their time. They will also abstain from giving feedback in the future. Plus, most will take the attitude that things are what they are at the organization and that they simply need to put up with it or leave. This is not a healthy mindset. It ends up magnifying any cultural challenges that exist. A feeling of helplessness breeds low people engagement, high-cost turnover, and poor productivity and product quality, and ultimately it negatively impacts your customer experience and top- and bottom-line business results.

Organizations need to ask their people for feedback regularly and take action based on that feedback to improve engagement and business outcomes. This is not optional in a high-performance culture. Asking the right questions and then having a solid process to share, discuss, analyze, and act on the feedback has a proven ROI that drives top- and bottom-line business results. In addition to the research I shared earlier, I personally saw it play out over my eleven years at Stryker. Thirty years of consecutive 20 percent EPS growth can't be argued with.

Most importantly, running a grassroots engagement initiative requires every person in your organization to take accountability for improvement and connects all your people to the bigger picture of fulfilling your organization's purpose. If people can't see the connection between what they do every day in their jobs and the meaning of the business, the value of their work is diminished, along with their engagement and performance. Instituting Purpose Meets Execution Action Planning into your business helps create this critical alignment.

If you have already asked your people for feedback using the Purpose Meets Execution process explained in Chapter 7, it is now time for action. Turning feedback into action is best done in a grassroots manner, at a team-by-team level. Doing this helps connect every person to the bigger picture through action rather than just words. If everyone is accountable for creating a high-engagement and high-performance culture, it is much more likely to happen. Plus, involving teams and individuals helps avoid the problem of the goal becoming some sort of forced HR initiative. It is a business initiative that everyone cares about because it produces a better place to work and a more successful and sustainable organization.

The key question you want everyone in your organization to answer for each statement proposed is what does "strongly agree" look like? The perfect balance between purpose and execution on the Purpose Meets Execution platform is "strongly agree" (6) for every response from everyone in your organization. While this would certainly be desirable, it is also an unrealistic expectation. No organization is perfect, and all low-scoring Purpose Meets Execution areas present an opportunity for improvement. Maintaining an organizational mean score of "somewhat agree" (5 or better) provides a very good foundation for a healthy business. Despite this, no organization should ever stop trying to reach the "strongly agree" (6) goal. While a perfect Purpose Meets Execution balance may remain elusive, all efforts in that direction improve people engagement and enhance business outcomes.

Purpose Meets Execution Action Planning Process

Purpose Meets Execution Action Planning is a way to openly share and discuss the feedback results and use the information to make and celebrate improvements. The process is simple and can easily be facilitated by an HR representative initially to guide remote or in-person team sessions. Managers with team Purpose Meets Execution mean scores (the aggregate average of all survey statement responses for that particular team) of "slightly disagree" or better (3+) can run their own sessions if they feel comfortable doing so. Ultimately, managers and leaders should be equipped to run their team's Purpose Meets Execution Action Planning session without assistance. However, when a team's Purpose Meets Execution mean scores are below "slightly disagree" (3), it is advisable to use a neutral facilitator who is not part of the team. This can be an HR representative or another trusted leader in the business.

Purpose Meets Execution Action Planning has very specific steps that should be followed initially to ensure effective first sessions. Once managers and leaders are comfortable facilitating the sessions, going off script is fine as long as the core objectives are met: sharing and discussing the team's Purpose Meets Execution mean scores for each statement asked, along with any relevant comments connected to the two open-ended questions. Finally, leaving the session with two to four team action items is key.

Ideally, I like Purpose Meets Execution Action Planning sessions to be scheduled for two hours. Less time can work, but do not schedule for less than one hour. If sessions can't occur in person, some form of video conferencing is preferable so people can read one another's eyes and body language. This may require the full two hours to ensure an active flow of dialogue and allow for any technology glitches or delays. As video and virtual reality technologies improve in the future, glitches will no longer be a factor. Teleconferencing can also work if other options are unavailable, but note that it is least effective because of other distractions that may exist for those calling in without a forced focus. In these cases, sharing a computer screen where real-time session notes are captured will help.

You will also want to electronically distribute all team scorecards and any comment roll-ups before the session. Managing a team in person or remotely—with or without a defined manager—requires strong and effective communication. This applies equally to multigenerational teams and the management of the Purpose Meets Execution Action Planning process. In all cases, leverage technology as much as possible to connect the eyes and faces of those who work for your organization to one another and ensure that communication is ongoing, consistent, understood, and meaningful.

When distributing and sharing Purpose Meets Execution team feedback, you must adhere to two important factors:

1. Never ask for or share Purpose Meets Execution feedback for teams that had fewer than five people participate in the survey. Doing so could compromise the anonymity of the feedback and cause people to lose trust in the process. If you use the Purpose Meets Execution tool found at PurposeMeetsExecution.com, only scorecards with five or more participants will be generated. If you use another third-party platform, you will need to ensure that it is set up this way and that no identifiable feedback is ever sent to your company.
2. Never distribute a response to an open-ended question that could identify the person offering the comment. In most cases, such comments will need to be scrubbed by someone in HR before the comments are distributed. Considering this, it is a good idea to

remind those participating in Purpose Meets Execution not to write anything that could identify them unless they want to be identified. Obvious identifiers such as name, exact position, or small office location should be avoided. HR may also want to consider removing others' names mentioned in open-ended responses if they are mean-spirited, inappropriately embarrassing, or libelous.

In any case, any alterations of participants' responses should be handled with great care and sensitivity. If people feel in any way inappropriately censored, they will lose trust in the process, and word will spread quickly. This will limit positive Purpose Meets Execution momentum and also negatively impact people engagement and trust.

The Purpose Meets Execution Action Planning steps are as follows.

Set the Tone

As the manager and/or facilitator, thank the group for participating and caring enough to respond to the Purpose Meets Execution survey. Assure the team that doing so will help make the organization an even better place to work for everyone and will help the business ultimately be more successful.

Explain that the intent of the session is to:

- Share and discuss the team's Purpose Meets Execution mean scores (overall and statement by statement), not how any single participant scored a particular statement. Discuss why participants may feel a particular statement was scored as it was. Assure everyone in the room, on screen, or on the phone that no one ever needs to share how she scored a particular statement and that no one will ever be asked.
- Share and discuss the team comments connected to the two Purpose Meets Execution open-ended questions. Again, no one should ever be asked to reveal who wrote what.

- Leave with two to four team action items to complete over the next six to twelve months.
- Discuss anything that might be on a team member's mind in a constructive and positive matter. It is not a complaint session.

Make everyone feel comfortable by pointing out that the intention of the session is to positively impact the engagement of the team and ultimately the future of the organization. It is important to openly and honestly discuss anything that may be on a person's mind in line with positive team and organizational improvements. Explain that the meeting is a safe place to discuss anything and that no retaliation will ever result from what people share during the session.

I also like to ask people to silence and put away any electronic devices that may cause distractions for them or others during the session.

> **Side note:** The more trust you have within the team, the better these sessions will go. If any manager or leader intentionally breaches the autonomy or trust of the Purpose Meets Execution Action Planning process, quickly removing that person from his people management role is advisable. Not doing so will put your whole culture of trust at risk.

Share Purpose Meets Execution Team Scorecard

As I mentioned in Chapter 7, any third-party platform you use to administer the Purpose Meets Execution survey must include the ability to generate team-by-team scorecards. These scorecards are for any team that has five or more survey participants. The scorecard should include each of the eleven Purpose Meets Execution statements and the mean score for each [i.e., strongly disagree (1) to strongly agree (6)]. It should also include the team mean score for all statements answered on the survey, plus a collection of all responses to the two Purpose Meets Execution open-ended survey questions. If you use the Purpose Meets Execution platform at PurposeMeetsExecution.com, this information plus other data points will automatically be included. Again, the Purpose Meets Execution process is about transparency and trust. Sharing this information openly fosters both.

Whether session participants have team scorecard printouts or electronic versions, everyone should have them available to view and to take notes on during the session.

Explain what the scorecards include and give everyone at least five minutes to look them over.

If your team had fewer than five participants, your session could use the next-level manager's team scorecard. Getting the team to openly and honestly discuss challenges and opportunities in your organization is ultimately most important.

Discuss Purpose Meets Execution Team Scorecard and Feedback

This is the heart of the Purpose Meets Execution Action Planning session. However, getting someone to start the discussion can be difficult. To overcome this, I ask the team questions like:

- Are there any surprises on the Purpose Meets Execution team scorecard?
- Any disconnects?
- What does a "strongly agree" (6) response look like to you for the overall team mean score or on a particular Purpose Meets Execution statement?

Ask for volunteers first, then pick someone to start if no one chooses to speak. I also use silence quite a bit to spur conversation. Ask a question and then stay silent until someone responds. People don't like to sit in silence, and 99.9 percent of the time someone will speak up. Allowing this silent space does take some practice, though. Sitting in silence is undeniably uncomfortable for most people.

Once the conversation gets going, use flip charts or a computer screen to capture thoughts from the team. Start with a general discussion and then move into more specifics after a team vote. If things come up that are well outside the scope and control of the team, acknowledge them but set them aside on a flip chart or elsewhere for another meeting and move on. Action planning sessions can easily get derailed. As the facilitator, keep the session on track with the goal of ending with two to four specific team actions to work on. I have found that sessions that run on and require additional meetings usually lose momentum at the second session. Keep one eye on the clock and ensure that the team leaves this session with next-step actions to be typed and sent to everyone soon after.

Take a Team Vote

Once you have had general discussions about the team's Purpose Meets Execution scores, it is time to focus all session participants on two statements team members are most interested in focusing on for further discussion. These statements can both be low scoring, both be high scoring, or be one of each. In all cases, the goal is to discuss the statements in line with positive actions that will result in a score closer to "strongly agree" (6) the next time the Purpose Meets Execution survey is administered. Any upward movement on any Purpose Meets Execution statement will yield improved team engagement and better business outcomes.

Ask those in the room to pick two statements they would most like to focus on over the next six to twelve months. This choice should include only the eleven Purpose Meets Execution ratable statements and not the two open-ended ones. It is helpful for people to think about where they believe their focus will bring about the most positive team change. You can either go around the meeting asking for everyone's top two statements or go statement by statement asking for a show of hands or positive response from people interested in working on the particular statement. Either way, the goal is to work on the two Purpose Meets Execution statements that have the most team member votes.

Once you have the team's top two Purpose Meets Execution statements to focus on, capture them on a flip chart, whiteboard, or screen for further discussion.

Consider an Action Plan

Now that you have the two Purpose Meets Execution statements of focus, you need to turn the team's discussion toward specific actions for each statement that would offer the biggest opportunity for team engagement. One or two actions per statement are sufficient. If the to-do list is too long, nothing will get done. In many cases, the action(s) your team implements connected to one statement will have a positive impact on another. For example, if the team completes an action (or actions) that improves people recognition in line with Purpose Meets Execution statement 6, most people will likely feel their work is making more of a difference to the organization's success, thereby improving the Purpose Meets Execution score for statement 9, too.

Look for low-hanging fruit wherever possible. These are the types of actions that are obvious, simple, and easy but have the greatest return on investment. For example, I once worked with a team that felt forgotten by the rest of the organization. They worked at a remote location without any of the extras people at headquarters enjoyed. A few hundred dollars for a Ping-Pong table, breakfast cereal bar, and beanbag chairs made the team feel valued, cared for, and listened to. Their engagement rose, and so did their productivity and work quality.

Try to keep actions as simple and focused as possible and within the team's control and influence. All discussions should center on what actions the team can take to improve their personal or team scores on the chosen statements, not those of other departments or the organization as a whole. The theory behind this is that if every team in the organization is going through the same exercise, team improvements will ultimately be organizational improvements.

Again, ask, "What does 'strongly agree' look like to you?" for the two statements. This will help the team focus on the appropriate actions to move the needle the next time the Purpose Meets Execution survey is administered.

Start by capturing all team thoughts on a flip chart, whiteboard, or screen.

Create Action Items

It is now time to take the notes you made from the general discussion around the two chosen statements and craft one or two SMART action items for each statement.

SMART stands for:

Specific: What the team is going to do stated in a simple and clear way. For example, meet as a team to discuss, draft, and adopt a team purpose statement that aligns with the organization's purpose by October 31.

Measurable: A measure that provides clear evidence of what the team accomplished. For example, if your team is working to improve its score on Purpose Meets Execution statement 6, it might decide that an action may be to recognize someone on the team or in the organization at each monthly meeting for exceptional work. Assuming there is one year before the next Purpose Meets Execution survey is administered, the measure for this item would be twelve instances of individual recognition. Measurements should be yes or no, with no gray area in between. Either the action was done or it wasn't.

Achievable: Something within the team's control and influence and doable within the time span between Purpose Meets Execution surveys—generally one year. Crafting an action plan that is too ambitious in conjunction with what might already be heavy workloads will lessen the possibility that it will get done. Actions should be impactful but reasonably achievable.

Results-focused: The return that your team will enjoy as a result of its efforts. For example, if your team decides to work on statement 8, the results of their action(s) may be improved internal or external customer satisfaction scores. If no such metric currently exists, part of the team's actions may be to create and administer a customer survey.

Time-bound: The timeframe in which your action will be completed. Again, set realistic and achievable goals. It is better to get something done over a longer period of time than to miss an aggressive target and never complete the action at all.

Avoid "manager to-do" lists. Purpose Meets Execution Action Planning is about the team, including the manager—not the manager on an island by herself. The manager might have some reasonable takeaways, but the list should be short and include only truly important items that may be beyond the control of others on the team.

Once one or two impactful SMART actions are drafted for each Purpose Meets Execution statement the team is working on, each statement needs a Purpose Meets Execution Action Leader assigned to it. In the best-case scenario, these are people on the team who volunteer for the post.

A Purpose Meets Execution Action Leader is the person responsible for ensuring that the actions get completed as specified and written by the team. However, the leader is not the person who does all the work. This important role is intended to give accountability to one person for the action's successful completion but may involve overseeing the work of others and delegating as needed. As the role's title suggests, it is a leadership position on the team connected to Purpose Meets Execution. This person should not be the manager of the team. Plus, the goal should be to involve as many people on the team as possible to successfully complete the action item. For example, the action item connected to statement 6 (previously mentioned) might suggest a rotation on the team to identify a different person each month who will recognize exceptional work. To ensure the recognition rotation continues to be meaningful, the action leader may require team members to come prepared with a story to illustrate the exceptional accomplishment they are recognizing.

If choosing such an action, don't make it a forced exercise. Recognition should always come from the heart. The key behind such an action is that people start to naturally look for good things going on in the business to report and point out to the team.

Explain Next Steps

Purpose Meets Execution is about accelerating people engagement and driving profits. Action is required for both goals. The team action plan needs to happen. Purpose Meets Execution Action Leaders must be held accountable for ensuring the plan gets done. And all team members should be accountable to support the initiatives, too.

Purpose Meets Execution is a grassroots cultural driver that requires the effort of everyone in the organization to build a great company and place to work. The more deeply this cultural tenet is embraced, the more like-minded people you will attract and retain. Those who don't buy in will start naturally selecting out on their own. A strong, consistent organizational culture is the best form of self-management.

To ensure accountability for getting promised Purpose Meets Execution actions completed, Action Leaders should report team Action Plan progress and updates to the whole team at least once a quarter. However, depending on the actions required, monthly updates may be more appropriate.

If your organization is using the Purpose Meets Execution survey platform, Action Leaders will also be required to update the Purpose Meets Execution Action Planning Tracker as needed. If you are using another third-party platform, it is advisable to at least track the progress of organizational Purpose Meets Execution Action Plans on a spreadsheet or in some other way.

Minimum Purpose Meets Execution Action Plan tracking and reporting should include the following:

- Team working on the statements
- Two team chosen statements

- Current team Purpose Meets Execution scores of the chosen statements
- Drafted actions connected to the statements
- Who the Purpose Meets Execution Action Leader is for each statement
- Quarterly progress updates

Celebrate Successes

When it comes to achieving important milestones or successes in a business, meaningful celebration is where many organizations fail. Despite the great things people accomplish, in a lot of cases, no one pauses to recognize their effort or even their big wins.

An important part of building Purpose Meets Execution momentum is meaningfully celebrating completed Purpose Meets Execution actions that have made a difference to the team or organization. When I say "meaningfully" I am not suggesting that the whole organization shuts down for the day or spends boatloads of money on a grand party. I am suggesting your organization makes sure that people know something good happened and that the efforts that went into achieving the great win are appreciated. This could be something as small as drinks at happy hour, a team lunch, or a short break in a meeting to recognize people. Most importantly, people need to know that what they suggested, worked on, and implemented was successful and valued.

By creating a process to celebrate improvements made as a result of Purpose Meets Execution feedback, people will feel good about the time they took to give the feedback. Also, they will build trust that the organization is listening to what people have to say and is acting on it, and they will be quicker to offer feedback the next time around.

One practice I used in the past is an internal people engagement website. Here, teams can post stories and pictures of organizational improvements connected to actions being completed. It is a powerful and effective way of spreading the good word and celebrating efforts.

When it comes to building positive Purpose Meets Execution momentum through celebration, poor initial survey scores can be a mixed blessing. It is not pleasant to receive them, but it is much easier to move the needle in the right direction quickly and significantly.

Measure Again

Once you have completed your first full cycle of Purpose Meets Execution, you will have established a foundational benchmark to build on—both with your organizational and team Purpose Meets Execution mean scores and your business results. With grassroots team Purpose Meets Execution focus, when you measure again in twelve months, you should see improvements in both, absent any unforeseen market condition changes.

"Strongly agree" (6) responses represent great organizational leadership. This should always be your organization's goal.

Key Purpose Meets Execution Action Planning takeaways are as follows:

- Participant survey responses are anonymous.
- Open and honest discussion about organizational challenges and opportunities is important.
- Two to four SMART actions are required for the two statements chosen by the team.
- All Purpose Meets Execution actions must be completed before the next time the Purpose Meets Execution survey is administered.

Chapter Questions

In line with your organization's Purpose Meets Execution Action Planning process, ask the following questions to ensure you are effectively embedding the process into your organization's cultural DNA.

- Has every team in my organization held a Purpose Meets Execution Action Planning session?
- Are all team Purpose Meets Execution Action Plans being tracked at an organizational level to ensure progress updates, plan completion, and score improvements?
- Has my organization captured both the Purpose Meets Execution organizational mean score and business results as a baseline for future measurement?
- Does my organization have a mindset of continuous improvement to drive team and organizational Purpose Meets Execution mean scores toward "strongly agree" responses?

PART III

Realizing a Winning Culture

CHAPTER 9

Bringing Purpose to Life

When you're surrounded by people who share a passionate commitment around a common purpose, anything is possible.

—Howard Schultz

Have you ever wanted to tell a really great story, a story so good you wanted the whole world to experience it? If so, you can relate to the world of a film producer. Film producers help bring stories to life with the goal of sharing them with as many people as possible. On the surface, their role may seem quite glamorous, perhaps with little to think about outside of spending money to create a film. But telling a story on film—while a momentous undertaking—is just the tip of the iceberg. The work that happens off the film set is often the most challenging, but it must be done if the producer is to share the film story with the masses. Lots of great films have been made that very few people have seen or even heard about.

Successful film producers share great stories with the masses by running great businesses. People know about their movies because they choose engaging stories, raise the needed money, hire the best talent, and market and sell their work effectively. Even ultra low-budget movies following a good business strategy can go mainstream. The 2009 movie *Paranormal Activity* was shot for just $15,000.[1] It had a unique online media campaign strategy that encouraged people to vote for the film to be shown in their area, as well as a marketing hook that involved "found footage." The film grossed nearly $197 million worldwide, producing an ROI of 655,000 percent.

To survive as a film producer, you must be able to execute effectively to get the movie made and then get paying audience members to watch what you have created and—if you play your cards right—buy any merchandise you can offer connected to it. In show "business," the more money you can raise or generate, the more people will be exposed to the story you are trying to share.

As a producer myself—mostly working in live theater—I learned the profit lesson the hard way. A comedy play I produced in New York City titled *Only You* by Timothy Mason had enough success to transfer from Off-Off Broadway to Off-Broadway in the mid-1990s. It ultimately received a favorable *New York Times* review. This should have ensured a bit of a run for the production and perhaps even a small profit. However, with my undergraduate degree in theatrical directing, my focus naturally drifted to the art side of the house. The *New York Times* reviewer liked what she had seen, but my lack of focus on the business side of the venture forced the production to close soon after.

I had good intentions. I chose to budget for a higher production value (sets, costumes, lighting, etc.), and forgo budget for box office personnel at the theater to sell tickets. My hope was to sell tickets exclusively through the ticket agency Ticketmaster. When the favorable *New York Times* review came out—after a painful two-week delay that required deferred compensation for the cast in order to keep the production running—the reviewer directed people to my locked theater instead of publishing Ticketmaster's phone number or web address. By the time I had discovered that people were milling around a dark box office window to buy tickets, it was too late, and my money ran out, much to the dismay of everyone involved in the production—my grandfather, several friends, and myself included—who lost our investments.

Only You was my first of many lessons spanning more than twenty years on the need to balance purpose and execution in a business. Too much of one and not the other creates poor or unfortunate outcomes. An organizational purpose must be met and brought to life with an equal portion of executional excellence. The best way to get this to happen is by spreading and reinforcing the word about what you and your organization are trying to do—its purpose.

How Are You Changing the World?

In October 2015, I was the keynote speaker at AAPEX, the world's largest auto care industry event, which attracts more than 150,000 people annually.

When most people think of this $500 billion industry, they think of wiper blades, washer fluid, cleaning supplies, oil cans, or the caps that cover the air valves on tires. They don't think about what would happen if the auto care industry were gone when they woke up in the morning. Where would they go to get their cars fixed? How would they safely get to work and back every day, drop off and pick up their children from school, enjoy family vacations, or transport loved ones to deliver babies? How would this affect the police officers and firefighters protecting communities and property who rely on seamlessly working vehicles? What about gardeners and sanitation workers who keep our neighborhoods and cities clean and maintained? Or construction personnel who build roads, buildings, and homes?

If the auto care industry vanished today, a good portion of movement on Earth would, too—and hundreds of thousands of jobs would disappear as well. It would be devastating to humanity.

Because auto care is an industry filled with older men, the focus of AAPEX 2015 was to attract new, diverse, and next-generation talent to an industry that needs to reinforce its important purpose.

If you know and understand how your organization or industry makes the world a better place, it is easier to spread the word and reinforce it. And by the way, 64 percent of millennials say this connection is a priority for them.[2] GE's current career opportunity commercials proclaiming, "Get yourself a world-changing job" makes this clear.[3]

How does my organization positively affect the lives of others? Knowing the answer to this important question is the first step to bringing your organizational purpose to life.

Executional Alignment

Ensuring that all those who work in your business can connect the purpose of your organization to what they do every day is the key to turning a soft concept like purpose into hard business results. Think of your people as the gears of a clock. If your purpose is to tell the time, every gear in the clock must be doing something specific to fulfill the clock's purpose. If one gear loses its connection to this purpose through misalignment, the entire clock fails. The more precise the gears' alignment, the more accurate the clock will be. The wrong gear, placement, or direction will stop time. This is how purpose is brought to life in an organization—through precisely aligned, exceptional execution.

Unfortunately, exceptional execution connected to an organization's larger purpose, especially on the front lines of a business, is often the exception. Many organizations get this wrong. Have you ever been in a retail store where the people working there ignore you when you need help? Do they not get that their job depends on your buying things there? Or have you run across a home service provider like a cable company that expects you to clear a four-hour window on a workday to wait for a serviceperson's arrival? Does the company not know that the only reason you can pay for the enjoyment of watching cable programs in your free time is because you work? Or perhaps, in the business-to-business space, you've encountered suppliers that do not seem to value on-time delivery. Do they not understand that your business may not be successful without the products they supply?

For commercial businesses, executional excellence means figuring out how everyone's job and daily duties connect to serving your organization's customers or clients. For not-for-profits, it means understanding how what a person does each day adds value to the cause of the organization and any fundraising efforts.

As simple as this concept is, it sometimes becomes clouded in practice, especially in the mid-levels of organizations. For example, in a tire dealership, it is easy to see that the person who puts the air in a tire or mounts it has a significant connection to customer safety and the purpose of the organization. If that worker gets it wrong, someone could die trying to get where he is going. After all, the tires of a speeding car are the only parts of the vehicle that actually touch the road. As we move up the chain of command, organizational purpose and the connection to daily work seem to disappear until they surface again at the senior levels of the organization. This may be due to a simple lack of thought or leaders who fail to make the connection. Despite this, the connections are there for every needed role in every organization—if you are asking the right questions and paying attention to the right things.

Take the tire dealership again. Who is managing those mounting the tires? If they are effective managers who engage their people, tire installers will care more about their jobs and see their importance. These managers will help connect the meaning for them. If the tire installer is actively disengaged, poorly managed, or unmanaged, he may not care if a lug nut is not tight enough or missing altogether.

In this case, the manager's role has an obvious impact on the organization's purpose. It comes to life when managers understand this and do their job well. The quote that "employees don't leave companies, they leave managers" is true and relevant. You can work in the best organization in the world under a poor manager or leader and go from being a stellar performer to being a poor and disengaged one. This organizational-level connection—manager to frontline contributor—applies across the board in all types of organizations. It breathes life into your organizational purpose.

The lack of clarity around connecting daily work to a larger purpose becomes even more strained at the department level. Support functions are labeled as cost centers—in most cases, spending money without making it. But what if decisions to expand manufacturing operations are made based on bad numbers from finance? What if IT employs poor technology that keeps bank customers from their money? Or what if HR fails to ensure a process to hire the right people or develop leaders and managers? In all cases, bottom-line results will suffer, limiting growth opportunity and an ability to drive an organizational purpose forward.

In the medical industry where I worked for eleven years, HR was critical to the organizational purpose of improving and saving lives. If exceptional talent wasn't coming in the door and staying, surgeons and patients would be at risk in operating rooms—in product quality, innovation, and support.

While the people directly serving your customers or clients are the ones closest to the organizational epicenter of purpose fulfillment, the same principle of connectivity applies up the organizational chain. Everyone's work in an organization—regardless of department, location, or level—is in some way connected to the larger purpose of the organization. If it is not, I would question whether the role is even needed or adds any value—or how it can be reconnected to the heart of the organization. Simply taking the time to think about the connection of your people's work to the larger goal and connecting the dots for all contributors brings organizational purpose to life.

In a story earlier in this book, a janitor in a NASA space center helped keep the workspace clean for those working to send a man to the moon. A dirty workspace can disengage, distract, or disorient people working on such an important project. It can also demonstrate a lack of care for people working at the organization. That's why the janitor's role was so crucial—and he knew it himself.

Every person in your organization must be able to see how his work connects to your larger organizational purpose and why what he does is important.

Arizona-based software company InfusionSoft actively encourages people working for the company to have side businesses to strengthen their connection to the organization's purpose of helping grow small businesses. By doing this, InfusionSoft is better serving its customers with a deeper understanding of their challenges and opportunities. This is a unified and coordinated focus across everything the company does.

A culture that embraces a one-team mentality ensures everyone is pulling in the same direction for a common purpose. Such organizations naturally break down silos and stay nimble as change is required.

Talent Alignment

I remember going over to my aunt and uncle's house when I was a child. My cousin Ben—who is eight years younger than I—was rarely around. He would spend most of his days in his room listening to sports on the radio. Ben has one of the biggest hearts of anyone I know. He is kind, warm, and soft-spoken. He comes off as extremely shy and quiet. To me, he is the definition of introverted. He frequently looks down when speaking with others and is consistently brief with his comments. Ben is definitely not one who appears to desire a place at the center of attention.

But as Ben grew, so did his interest in sports. He played high school football at University High School in Irvine, California, and was a sports broadcaster for the Saddleback College Gauchos men's basketball and football games on KSBR before landing a job as an AM sports radio journalist.

When I was living in New York City, Ben came to visit me. I had not seen him in a while and didn't know much about his career, other than that he was involved in the sports world. Ben invited me to a Mets baseball game he was covering. When I arrived, I was escorted to the press box area where Ben met me. We sat perched above the playing field just off first base. Ben was seated in front of a large microphone as we caught up on things. With his usual demeanor, he spoke warmly and softly—using few words—as his eyes shifted from me, to the ground, and to the field.

When the game began, Ben turned to the microphone and lit up. And I am not talking a few points on a scale here. I am talking ten thousand points! The tone of his voice became energetic, confident, and powerful.

He was funny, focused, and quick-witted. He knew every single fact about every single player and the game of baseball. I sat there in utter amazement as I watched him call the game. He was flawless and engaging. I felt like I had witnessed a superhero transformation. It was marvelous. From that day on, Ben not only personified for me what being aligned with what you do best in life looks like but also what it means to be aligned in a career that feeds your personal purpose. Ben is alive behind a microphone. No one does it better than he does.

After cohosting the *Ben & Dave Show* on XTRA Sports 1150 in Los Angeles, hosting *Dodger Talk*, and being a regular contributor to the NBC Sports Network, Benjamin "Big Ben" Maller is now a celebrated American sports radio host for Fox Sports Radio.[4] He is also credited with being one of the original sports bloggers and helping Fox Sports' website overtake ESPN.com in unique visitors for the first time in February 2007. In 2011, Ben gave live updates on the Tōhoku earthquake and tsunami from a caller who had called in to his show and was living in the area.

My cousin is an example of how purpose can come to life in an organization with correctly aligned people. He's also a great example of the results that follow. He even has menu items named after him in various restaurants around the United States.

For people to deliver optimum results for your organization, they must be in a role that plays to their natural strengths, like my remarkable cousin Ben.

Values

Dan Henkle, president of Gap Foundation and SVP of global sustainability for the retailer Gap, attributes his twenty-five-year career at the company to a connection to the organization's values that feed the organization's purpose. Henkle says Gap's values have everything to do with the way it does business and how the company treats its people. "It extends beyond our own workforce to suppliers, the community we work in, and how we play an important part in society. It makes you want to stay with the company through thick and thin," Henkle explains.

Company values support an organization's ability to fulfill its purpose if they are lived by the organization. If you value empowerment—you talk about it and put it on the walls—but in reality, you practice micro-management, there is a disconnect. Any disconnect between the values of a business and its actions chips away at the foundation of your organization—and ultimately at its ability to fulfill its purpose.

To ensure your values support what you are trying to do, you need to start with why your business was started in the first place. If a value does not support your intentions, it should not be embraced.

For example, a technology company had better value innovation and creativity. A company in the service industry must value serving others. For a holiday travel agency, valuing leisure time and exploration is key. For an airline or auto manufacturer, safety is paramount. For all leadership, integrity is foundational.

Ensuring that you are aligning your organizational values with what you stand for as a business ensures that everyone is focused on the right things—from your people to your top leadership to your customers.

Care

Woody Allen once said, "Eighty percent of success is showing up." He may be right, but it is the other 20 percent that really matters. To bring purpose to life in your organization, you need people who go well beyond showing up. You need people who care deeply about what you do and feel cared for, too.

Even if you effectively align work, talent, and values to your organization's purpose, your business will never truly come alive unless the people in your business honestly care about your company and what it needs to do for customers, the community, and the world.

Kevin Cleary, CEO of Clif Bar & Company, states it this way:

> People with purpose drive performance. To that end, it's important to recognize that people are not inspired by the quantity of a company's profits—what they care about and what inspires them is the opportunity to have a positive impact in the world; to do meaningful work. As a family- and employee-owned, purpose-driven company, the success of our business execution relies on the connection our people feel to the company's goals of sustaining our business, brands, people, community, and the planet. This connection . . . it's what inspires our people to share their best with us and each other.

To help people connect with Clif Bar & Company's goals and bottom line—what the company calls its Five Aspirations—the organization has created a program called White Road Expeditions. A two-day experiential development program with several months of coaching support, White Road Expeditions helps people map out their personal and professional development goals and identify areas where they can connect their personal values to the goals of the company. Through this program, the company has seen people deepen their connection to the organization's purpose while charting paths to new directions for personal and professional goals.

One example of the program's success is Suzy Starke German, the company's women's experience manager for LUNAFEST, Clif Bar's organization that showcases talented female filmmakers sharing their stories and causes through film. At White Road Expedition in January 2013, German committed to adopting a child that year, and eight months later her son, Jasper, arrived.

She said White Road Expeditions enabled her to commit in writing to her priorities and share them with colleagues at her table. When you do that, there's a real intentionality to a commitment. She said it was very special to have a work forum that gave her permission to say her top priority could be her family, while still being dedicated to her job. It showed that you don't have to separate the personal and professional at Clif Bar.

What's more, Clif Bar's adoption benefit—$10,000 per child for up to two children—made it financially possible for German and her husband to afford the adoption process so quickly a second time. Their first adopted child, also facilitated with Clif Bar's adoption benefit, wasn't even a year old at the time.

"At Clif Bar, we exist to feed and inspire adventure. Adventure is about connecting to things that we love, trying new things, and stretching ourselves as individuals. This is not just something that we want for the people who eat our food, it's also what we want for our people—and it doesn't have to just exist on a Saturday or Sunday. I want employees who are fired up, energized, and inspired. I want them to bring their best selves to Clif Bar every day . . . their whole selves," Cleary adds.

To do this, Clif Bar wants its people to bring their "love-tos" to work. Whether it's using company time to volunteer at an organization they care about, working out in the gym, going for a bike ride, or even playing music in the company band, the company has found that the secret to productivity isn't gluing people to their desks, it's inspiring them to step away from them and even paying them to do it.

Stories

KPMG is one of the Big Four auditors and public accounting firms, alongside Deloitte, Ernst & Young, and PricewaterhouseCoopers. The firm's clear purpose is to ensure the integrity of information on which stakeholders, the investor community, the capital markets, and individual investors in 401k plans base their financial decisions regarding public companies. "That's what a public company audit does," shares Bruce Pfau, vice chair of human resources and communications at KPMG.

While the perception of an organization filled with accountants might be dull, KPMG is anything but. It is an organization filled with approximately 174,000 passionate people who know they are making a difference in the world. “We don’t ask people to memorize a slogan about the purpose of our firm, but rather ask them how they fit into it,” Pfau says. “In a grassroots manner, we allow people to express their meaning and purpose to the work they do instead of imposing one.” To do this on a grand scale, Pfau created what he called the 10,000 Story Challenge, asking people at the firm to share their purpose in a framed poster. “It is a grassroots way of asking our people ‘What do you do at KPMG?’” Pfau explains.

In June 2014, John Veihmeyer, the global chairman and CEO of the firm, announced the challenge, with an incentive of two extra days of paid vacation if ten thousand stories were received by Thanksgiving. Stories flooded in, including comments like “I promote peace” and “We protect our nation.” By the time Thanksgiving rolled around, more than forty thousand stories had been submitted. “The participation far exceeded our expectations and our engagement scores soared to historic highs,” Pfau says. And in fact, 86 percent of the firm’s U.S. employees agreed that KPMG was a great place to work.

The power of sharing stories to ignite purpose goes far beyond an internal engagement score record. It has a direct impact on business operations and customer engagement. The firm had its most profitable year in its 118-year history. “Fulfilling our firm’s higher purpose has enabled us to achieve exceptional financial performance,” Pfau proudly explains.

Personal stories are a way of elevating the purpose of your people in their own words. It captures how their work impacts their teammates, customers, and society at large. “We asked people to look at their work from a different angle and perspective. To see the end result of what they do each day and the meaning it has to others, rather than us telling them what it should look like. I think top-down communications are important as well, but most firms leave it at that. We were encouraging our people to be actively engaged, bottom up,” Pfau says.

The other interesting revelation that Pfau noticed in KPMG’s challenge results is that, contrary to conventional wisdom, it is not only millennials who care about purpose in their careers and jobs. Everyone cares about these crucial things, people of all ages and backgrounds.

Engaging people around purpose is in KPMG's cultural DNA. "We have very few leaders or partners who say, 'Why focus on this stuff? We just need to push our people harder,'" Pfau says.

> There's not a leader in the firm that doesn't accept as a matter of fact and faith that being an employer of choice is a business advantage. We don't need to do lots of studies to tell us that. Our deep belief, understanding, and engagement in what we are doing is our differentiator.

KPMG's story around purpose is also part of its external employment brand. The company's recruiting websites and hiring processes all support the purpose-based culture it has built. "People know what matters to us," Pfau says. "People we're considering hiring know what we are about based on what we present to them and what they hear in the marketplace. There's a certain amount of self-selection."

"We have a fairly rigorous selection process. It is a very collaborative and team-oriented process. It takes a very long time to get hired here," Pfau adds.

Cultural fit is non-negotiable at KPMG. Anyone hired must buy into the firm's purpose and core values. Like all company cultures, one size does not fit all. However, considering that KPMG hires about seven thousand people a year, it has a remarkable track record, with a high-performer turnover of only 7 percent.

Many corporate environments are guilty of telling stories that appeal exclusively to people's heads, engaging their commercial sensibilities or their cognitive, logical side. Clearly, this needs to happen at some level. "But I think we also miss appealing to people's hearts as well. An organizational anthem that evokes an emotional reaction, a tear in people's eyes, chokes them up in some way," Pfau says. This is not about manipulating people. Instead, it is akin to creating a great piece of art or literature that appeals to a deeper sense of emotion—a subtext that cannot be seen but is felt.

"People who are emotionally tethered to an organization can't think of working at any other place. That's what separates good from great. We want our people to feel they just heard 'The Star-Spangled Banner,' not teach them the structure and objectives of writing national anthems. It's the difference between the heart and the head," Pfau explains.

Like KPMG, O.C. Tanner is an organization that uses stories to bring its organizational purpose to life. David Sturt, EVP of marketing, says, "We found the most accurate assessment of the way a culture really operates is the sum total of the stories that are shared and told around particular values or belief systems. It is a very powerful facilitator reminding people of our purpose. Stories about our people, our customers, what people are doing, how, and where bring our purpose to life."

Not surprisingly, O.C. Tanner uses recognition to help empower and create organizational stories. It makes a practice of recognizing exceptional people's efforts in line with the company's organizational purpose and sharing the stories with others. Sturt adds:

Inevitably, we'll have a customer call us late in the afternoon and they'll say "Oh my gosh, we're doing this recognition event tomorrow, the CEO is going to be there, we have everything planned, and we completely forgot about one of the key members of the team who is being recognized. Is there any way you can make an award to present to them tomorrow?" And I can't tell you how many times somebody says, "I'll get it there," finds a way to get the award made, packaged up, and catches a flight that night to ensure our customer is able to recognize the person in the morning. These stories get told around the company. It becomes part of the fabric of our culture. Nothing carries a greater sense of humanity and authenticity than stories of people doing real things connected to fulfilling the purpose of the organization.

"The person who got on a red-eye, gave up their night and turned around and came back the next day—my goodness, we are going to recognize that person. And that's core not only because it's exactly what we are about, but we also believe that's an essential part of helping [to] prove that we value when people actually live our values and purpose," Sturt declares.

When people are actually changing their actions and behaviors to align with your organization's purpose, it is absolutely imperative that you recognize it, Sturt advises. Not doing so is detrimental to living purpose in an organization. "It becomes this really powerful litmus test that every employee wants to know. Is this real or just a bunch of hype handed down from senior leadership?" Sturt adds.

When people hear stories of exceptional and purpose-aligned work getting recognized throughout the organization, authenticity is reinforced. When people really feel that everyone—at all levels of the organization—truly cares about living an organizational purpose, it comes to life, creating sustainability and business success.

Chapter Questions

To bring purpose to life in your organization, you need to ensure people alignment with execution, talent, values, care, and stories. Asking and answering the following questions will help you assess your organization's gaps.

Execution:

- Do people in my organization know how they make (or raise) money for my organization?
- Do people in my organization know how they help control costs for my organization?

Talent:

- What percentage of people in my organization are doing what they do best at least 80 percent of the time?

Values:

- Are my organization's values supporting what my organization is trying to achieve?

Care:

- What percentage of people working in my organization care about what they do more than their paychecks?
- What percentage of people working in my organization feel their personal purpose is aligned with that of the organization?

Stories:

- Does my organization regularly share and recognize its exceptional people and customer purpose-aligned stories?

Notes

1. "10 Most Profitable Low Budget Movies of All Time." *Business Pundit*, April 4, 2011. www.businesspundit.com/10-most-profitable-low-budget-movies-of-all-time/11/.
2. Rob Asghar. "What Millennials Want . . ." www.forbes.com/sites/robasghar/2014/01/13/what-millennials-want-in-the-workplace-and-why-you-should-start-giving-it-to-them/#2c300c392fdf (cited in footnote 2).
3. "What's the Matter with Owen?" *GE*. https://www.youtube.com/watch?v=3xGoBlI_fdg&feature=youtu.be.
4. "Ben Maller." *Wikipedia*. https://en.wikipedia.org/wiki/Ben_Maller.

CHAPTER 10

Keeping Your Promises

I'm not upset that you lied to me. I'm upset that from now on I can't believe you.

—Friedrich Nietzsche

Consistently keeping your promises is about executional excellence. It is your *what* in your organization's *why*, *where*, and *what* that I discussed in the opening of this book. It means your organization takes the appropriate actions to ensure it does what is says it is going to do when it said it would do it. This includes business expectations such as product launch timings, quality, budget attainment, sales and profit forecasts, and ultimately shareholder or stakeholder value. It also includes promises made to people working in your business. Promises broken represent trust lost. Lost trust creates retention and engagement issues, reduced customer spending and customer loss, and adverse investment decisions like selling or shorting traded stock or not investing at all.

I was blessed to grow up in HR at Stryker Corporation. In all my career travels and experiences, I have yet to find an organization more dedicated to the development and engagement of its people than Stryker. During my eleven-year career at the company, I saw massive investment of time, money, and resources dedicated to hiring the right people for the right roles and engaging and developing those people globally. There was never a strategic business decision made at the company that didn't start and finish with a conversation about people. As the divisional head of HR for various global locations, I was involved in all general business meetings, along with the head of finance and the divisional president. From these meetings and watching Stryker operate globally, I learned what good business execution looks like and how having the right people practices in place makes it all work. Keeping promises at Stryker meant hitting intended targets.

The attention built into the core of Stryker around people placement, development, engagement, and executional excellence delivered a remarkable 20 percent annual growth for thirty years. It is an impressive and historic track record. This was done by keeping promises internally and externally through superb execution in an effort to ultimately improve the lives of people. The mantra "20 percent forever," driven by former CEO John Brown, was coupled by patient visits to manufacturing sites and meetings so people working on, marketing, and selling the products knew the impact of their work.

The words of people whose lives were saved or improved as a result of what Stryker does left few dry eyes in the audience. There were younger patients receiving a second chance at life after a terrible accident or disease, and older ones who could now play golf again without pain or lift a grandchild into their arms for a hug. I witnessed hand finishers, people who put tiny beads on implants, and those who packaged the products tear up. It was always powerful and reinforced the importance of strong execution in everything we did, from the quality of our product, to on-time delivery, to new innovations, to making life even better for people. It is all tied firmly together into one machine built on purpose. Keeping promises at Stryker is not only important to the people who work there but critical to the lives of people they serve.

The way Stryker runs its business is a powerful example of how companies can connect even the most basic routine work to a larger organizational purpose and achieve enhanced execution, fueled by a tremendous amount of accelerated people engagement. When people feel their work is meaningful, they work harder, produce better results, are more efficient, and care more about what they're doing. This translates into higher-quality products, happier and more loyal customers, and improved business results.

Another execution alignment practice at Stryker can be observed as you walk through the halls of the company offices. Pictures and videos of patients are displayed throughout. They serve as strong reminders to the people who work at the company that the work they do is important to others.

Whether you are selling software to a business to help them be more profitable or selling trauma products to hospitals to allow accident victims to walk again, you are positively impacting the lives of others. In this context, keeping promises matters more when you know other people are relying on you for their success or well-being. It also helps keep people and the business focused on the right tasks and eliminates waste from their to-do lists. From my experience, I can safely say that 80 to 90 percent of the items on corporate to-do lists don't add true value to the business or support fulfilling the organization's purpose. Staying focused on the end result of why you are executing on a certain task helps keep focus where it needs to be. It also supports people in your business, so they can hold one another accountable for spending time, effort, and resources wisely.

Understanding and communicating the impact that people throughout your business make on others through their ability to execute effectively is the difference between mediocre, good, and great work. Being part of Stryker's growth from about $1 billion in 2000 to more than $8 billion a decade later, and from a few thousand people to nearly twenty-four thousand, offered me a front-row seat to the way organizations keep promises and fulfill their purpose both internally and externally.

An Organization Built Around Keeping Promises

National Life Group is an organization built around keeping promises. Its core business is life insurance, but it also offers annuities, mutual funds, and other financial services.[1] In 2015, its revenue was $1.8 billion. For more than 165 years, National Life has insured everyone from celebrities to working people, including passengers on the *Titanic* and *Hindenburg* and victims of the great influenza epidemic of 1918–1919. Chartered by the Vermont Legislature on November 13, 1848, National Life began selling policies in 1850. Its first claim came only months later.

Rowland Allen of Ferrisburgh, Vermont, bought two life insurance policies worth $500 each before heading out to find gold and riches in California. Unfortunately, Allen died of dysentery just before completing his journey.

National Life, having just opened its doors for business, didn't yet have the cash on hand to pay Allen's widow the $1,000. In a remarkable demonstration of commitment to keeping the organization's promises in line with its purpose, "to bring peace of mind," its directors and officers put their personal credit on the line and worked with a local bank to pay the claims.

To put this deed in perspective, $1,000 in 1850 would be worth approximately $30,303 today. Considering workers earned an average of about 90 cents a day back then, this was a significant amount of money.

Keeping promises is crucial to National Life's purpose of giving customers peace of mind and is absolutely core to what the company does. Imagine an insurance company that had a record of fulfilling only 90 percent of its legitimate claims. That number may seem high until you think about the 10 percent of people who bought policies, only to leave their loved ones destitute when they died. Or of those who purchased living benefit insurance and then found themselves with no money to pay bills when a debilitating illness struck. No one would take a risk with such an organization. "Bringing peace of mind" requires that the company always keeps its promises by executing on every policy sold. Not doing so would quickly force it out of business. Executional excellence is mandatory at National Life and is intimately connected to the purpose of the company. Mehran Assadi, the president and chief executive officer of National Life, says, "We are in the business of making promises that need to be fulfilled thirty, forty, fifty, sixty, seventy, or, believe it or not, eighty years from now. Our business is about the fulfillment of promises, short- and long-term."

National Life's commitment to keeping its promises goes far beyond paying off policies. It extends to their people, agents, customers, and community. With 98 percent Glassdoor approval of the CEO and 87 percent of employees who rated the organization on Glassdoor saying they would recommend the company to a friend, there is clear evidence of trust and engagement at National Life.

The company has consistently paid a dividend on its participating life insurance policies every year since 1855. Through the Civil War, the Great Depression, two World Wars, and, most recently, the Great Recession, National Life has delivered. Its life insurance sales have doubled since 2011 and its customer base continues to grow, from 796,000 in 2014 to 843,000 in 2016.

When National Life speaks about its ability to execute on bringing peace of mind to others, it focuses on its *what*: to create a better future for each and every client through innovative financial solutions and by keeping every promise. This is what every person working at National Life focuses on every day. If the company gets this right, it will achieve its vision and purpose of "bringing peace of mind to everyone they touch." If National Life gets it wrong, customers and their loved ones may suffer.

"Our industry, in my opinion, is misunderstood. We do a lot of good for our customers and communities," Assadi says. Six years ago, National Life revisited its values, and under Assadi's leadership the company's focus became, "Do good. Be good. Make good." "These values represent our intentions, actions, and outcomes, respectively," Assadi adds.

The values mantra was communicated and socialized with associates and agents of National Life—twenty thousand people strong across fifty states. At some point, there was a debate between the words "good" versus "great." Good was ultimately chosen due to a belief that people in the insurance industry and at National Life tend to be "do-gooders," Assadi says. "Our philosophy is that people want to be part of something important and serve a real cause. Our job is not to sell things. Our job is to educate and create awareness that life happens. And no one can predict, as far as life is concerned. So how do you bring assurance, not insurance, into the picture?" Assadi asks. This is where keeping promises through superb execution matters most.

"I wonder how many people die with the dignity they deserve. That's what we're bringing into the picture. You have no choice but to get passionate and juiced up about how personal this industry is and why, at National Life Group, we describe ourselves as a purpose-driven company," Assadi says.

Assadi speaks of making sure that people who are part of National Life understand the *why* of what they do. His focus is not what most would expect from the CEO of an insurance company. Most in his industry focus on *what* and *how*, not *why*. "And if you are trying to inspire a team to reach for a higher cause, you need to emphasize the *why* and start communicating and branding it inside out," Assadi affirms.

"Forget about all that other stuff," Assadi says. "What is the right thing to do? It's very simple stuff. It comes down to execution. Are you living it or are you showing it in pedantic ways?" Execution for a higher cause must be in the fabric of your organization to keep you pointed in the right direction. "It can't be about commissions. If you are doing the right thing for your clients, everything else will work," Assadi confirms.

When you continuously socialize the connection between keeping promises and a higher purpose in large groups, small groups, and one on one, at some point everyone starts talking in that kind of a way. "And that's the time a leader just needs to get the hell out of the way because the genie is out of the bottle and it is bigger than any individual," Assadi adds.

At the heart of making good on promises is achieving your business objectives. Behind every corporate promise is a balance sheet. At National Life, the objective is capital, top-line growth, and net income. Instead of talking about its liabilities, the company speaks about the promises it is making. This subtle change in language represents a drastic departure from the way most companies view their balance sheets. It makes what they are living in the organization real in every sense—from the finance department to every other department and person, everyone is there to "keep promises" in order to "bring peace of mind."

At National Life, profitability is a four-letter word, LOVE: "Leading Our Values Every Day." The idea is to give value to customers and fair compensation to agents and associates. The model has helped the company to grow its capital organically through engagement. Growing its capital allows it to continue to make promises to its customers and serve its communities. It backs up the promises to families, business owners, and the communities the company is a part of.

Another key to getting this right is simplicity. "We are the king of making things so complex even out of something simple," Assadi says. One of the mantras National Life has this year is, "Simple is hard." According to Assadi, it will probably remain the battle cry for the next three years. How do you simplify it? Get the dumb out of the process? Create something better? Lower unit costs? Improve returns? These will be the questions asked by those at National Life in order to earn the right to take care of customers who are underinsured or who have no insurance at all.

"We are about being progressive and efficient," Assadi says.

> I believe what is measured gets improved, and to that end, I believe what separates great organizations from average ones is lots of execution. Too many in business claim to be visionaries and are poor implementers, and that's what we put front and center first.

National Life measures its executional success first through the eyes of its customers. What is the customer experience the company is providing? Are customers providing positive feedback and continuing their relationship with the company? The company uses surveys to measure how it is handling new and existing business. Screens in National Life's offices capture key customer matrices, showing how the company takes care of their needs and supports them.

Keeping promises also requires that you have the right products to sell. In 2008, some things blew up in the insurance industry. Seeing the writing on the wall, National Life stayed away from certain product offerings. Assadi's decisions were not always popular at the time, but he stuck to his guns, saying: "If I cannot understand it and I cannot see the customer value, I'm not going to sell it. If I'm not going to get the proper return, I'm not going to build it and I'm going to stay away from it." According to Assadi, a lot of promises were being made in 2005–2007 that came undone in 2008. This was the result of irresponsible products that couldn't be executed on. "After 2008, people thought we were geniuses, but we weren't. If you don't understand something, stay away from it. Stick to your knitting, at what you're good at, versus just chasing top line," Assadi advises.

Keeping promises also requires a strong culture made up of people who believe what your organization believes. Misalignment will cause people to stray from the important work that needs to get done. Not everyone who wants to be an agent for National Life becomes one. Decisions to hire are based heavily on a person's cultural fit and alignment with the organization's purpose. The company has a practice of rejecting potential agents even when there are immediate opportunities for top-line growth based on existing relationships. Long term, the company knows the decision is not right and walks away.

"Pilots have airtime. In our industry you have street time. It's not an easy industry, but it's a worthy industry because you are positively impacting the lives of so many people. Your legacy as a person working for or with us is [that] you may be dead and gone, but the work you have done continues to impact many lives and many families," Assadi concludes.

Johnny Promises

Johnny "Cupcakes" Earle[2] built a company around design and execution. His clothing brand focuses mainly on T-shirts with the company's logo, a skull and crossbones, with a cupcake silhouette replacing the skull, prominently displayed on the front. Company designers often incorporate other elements that replace iconic symbols, like the torchlight on the Statue of Liberty, with cupcakes. If T-shirts are not your thing, there are also branded hats, leggings, duffle bags, totes, socks, air fresheners, pins, key chains, and even cans of fake cake frosting.

The Massachusetts-based company sells its uniquely designed products online and out of old-fashioned "bakeries" with no food. At these locations, you will find antique baking racks, refrigerators, wood-burning ovens, and vanilla air fresheners hidden behind the air vents to create a bakery smell. Products are displayed on baking trays and inside glass pastry cases. Store windows read, "No sugar! No carbs! No fat!" Considering that the company is a clothing business, this is all true.

Once, the company released a limited-edition breakfast T-shirt that was available only until noon. The marketing gimmick was poking fun at fast-food restaurants that refuse to sell breakfast items even one minute past their advertised cutoff time. One customer who drove from New York to Boston to buy a bright yellow T-shirt that substituted its crossbones with bacon and a butter knife showed up a few minutes after 12:00 p.m. and was politely turned away.

Good or bad, Johnny Cupcakes' brand keeps its promises, even when it has to forgo a sale.

"My concept is strange. Strange is good. Strange is important. It sets you apart from the rest," Earle says. But that's true only if you are effectively executing to deliver on your brand promises, as Earle has consistently done since founding his "bakery" in 2001 out of the trunk of his car.

On Fridays at noon (EST), the company releases new T-shirt designs or other products. Customers have slept on the sidewalk in front of his stores for days to get the next creation. Once supplies of limited-edition products run out, that particular design is never again reproduced. To buy one of Johnny Cupcakes' T-shirts, you can expect to pay anywhere from $35 to $60 or more. If you wait until after limited-edition supplies sell out, a T-shirt could cost you upward of $100 to $500 on eBay.

Earle's attention to detail is his secret ingredient. Even T-shirt labels are consistent with his brand, shaped like tiny oven mitts. His designs are unfailingly unique and creative, and he always delivers what he promises, from store openings, to product releases, to packaging and other surprises. He's done things like including a Barbie doll's head, batteries, or a handwritten note with an order to make customers feel special. Earle's goal is to make his customers feel like it is their birthday when they purchase a product. All items come in packaging that would normally contain some form of edible treat. The appliances in his stores have oven doors that open and close on their own and emit steam at random intervals. Even the knobs twist and turn. Johnny Cupcakes promises his customers an experience that needs to be delivered with every transaction.

Johnny Cupcakes is a rapidly growing multimillion-dollar movement. The company even boasts more than two thousand fans with the brand logo tattooed on various parts of their bodies. No pressure to continue to keep its promises!

Finding Leaders Who Keep Promises

Finding great purpose-driven leaders who can effectively drive execution at a high level is both an art and a science. The art can be navigated by using the purpose recruitment tools I have outlined earlier in this book. The science comes with having a good process to recognize leaders who keep their promises through executional excellence.

When Cher Murphy, chief talent officer at the Institute of Corporate Productivity and an expert in placing successful leaders at top organizations, speaks about hiring and assessing leaders, she divides them into two categories: builders and extenders.

Builders are leaders who have created a new organization from a start-up or led a large transformation, including M&A work—a key indicator of being able to meld culture, purpose, systems, and work teams.

Those who have successfully led in such environments are traditionally great executors by nature.

Murphy notes, "In search, we have simplified this by saying, 'Builders can be identified easily when asked if they saw a burning building would they run toward it, finding an immediate solution, or run to get help from the fire department, relying on a framework that experts have created. Those who run towards the building are most likely your executors. Those who go for help are your extenders."

An excellent leadership candidate would call the fire department as she headed toward the building.

Using successful candidate profiles based on leaders currently in your business is helpful, but using predictive analytics in this way becomes more challenging at senior levels. However, this process, when combined with innovative purpose-based search techniques, can produce great results.

Hiring leaders who can effectively execute begins with a deep understanding of the company's direction, culture, values, vision, and purpose. Plus, you must keep in mind the specific outcomes that this leader will need to execute on within the first six to twelve months and the next five to ten years in the role. Even if the organization's intention is to rotate the leader into other roles in the shorter term, placing leaders for long-term, sustainable success is the mindset to lead with. Any results in the short term must be connected to the long-term big picture of fulfilling the organization's purpose. Results considered exclusively in terms of short-term gains can be detrimental to sustainability.

The ability of a leader to execute at a high level can be tied to multiple characteristics and specific experiences. "Many search consultants or internal talent acquisition leaders focus on specific companies to find a specific talent. Across industries, there are marquee companies that have strong reputations of excellence in specific roles: Blackrock for investment management leaders, PepsiCo for HR talent, and Google for software engineers," Murphy says.

The breakdown of this traditional method of search comes from these organizations' valuing certain leadership styles and a specific skill set.

Plus, the leader develops a unique history and experience with mergers and acquisitions and transformations that these marquee companies have navigated.

"Mergers and acquisition experience provides leaders the ability to show traditional leadership skills like designing a new organization, merging systems to create efficiencies, focusing on effectiveness, or driving bottom-line results," Murphy adds.

The people-centric and communication skills needed to effectively create organizational change are vital. Many business leaders can walk you through theories of executing on the merger of two different organizations, but doing it successfully is a whole other matter. "The insights gained from having a leadership candidate walk you through the successes and failures they've encountered leading a merger and acquisition can clarify their skill set and highlight their ability to keep promises and get things done," Murphy says.

"Thorough candidate interviews and assessments, a broad and deep understanding of the talent marketplace, and a clear grasp of the organization's purpose and what they are trying to do short and long term all contribute to finding operationally excellent talent that can deliver executional excellence to a business," Murphy concludes.

Chapter Questions

Ensuring your organization keeps its promises—internally and externally—and has leaders who can drive and deliver executional excellence to fulfill an organizational purpose is critical to the success and sustainability of a business. You can assess your organization's level of execution by asking and answering the following questions. Ask other business colleagues and your customers as well.

- Does my organization always follow through on its promises to others and me?

- As a customer, would I (or do I) feel that the organization always keeps its promises?
- Does my organization practice what it preaches?
- Do the leaders in my organization consistently do what they say they will do?

Note

1. "Our Story." *National Life Group*. https://www.nationallife.com/OurStory-OurHistory.
2. See www.johnnycupcakes.com and @JohnnyCupcakes on Twitter.

CHAPTER 11

Getting the Balance Between Purpose and Execution Right

So be sure when you step. Step with care and great tact and remember that Life's a Great Balancing Act.

—Dr. Seuss

Once your organization has a clear understanding and belief in its *why*, *where*, and *what*, all attention must be turned to getting the balance right between its focus on what it wants for its customers, community, or the world and what it needs to do every day to meet that goal. Like a ballerina's center light that keeps her from falling over as she spins gracefully on stage, your organization's focus on where it is going will ground and guide its efforts—ensuring that it is facing the right direction and won't fall over.

Walking the Tightrope

When Philippe Petit floated 1,350 feet in the air between New York City's beloved Twin Towers in 1974, he was balancing on a steel cable without a net or safety wire. He astonished spectators below for forty-five minutes with the ultimate demonstration of purpose and execution. Petit passed eight times between the two towers—smiling, dancing, kneeling, and even lying down on the wire. Despite having to surrender to waiting police after his finale, he became an instant global sensation. Petit was clearly born to entertain and inspire people to achieve the seemingly impossible as a tightrope walker.

While Petit had his challenges and mishaps along the way, his ultimate goal was achieved in a grand way. His attention to detail and ability to execute on an intense and strategic preparation plan helped mitigate any last-minute hiccups that could have derailed his efforts.

Like Petit, organizations must have a clear purpose and vision of what they are trying to do and what that ultimate goal looks like when they arrive. An organization must then be able to connect the actions it needs to take, step by step, to get there—short and long term.

While Petit's focus was on executing one step at a time on his tightrope, six years of planning, research, observation, and preparation went into executing what he called the "artistic crime of the century."

Balancing One Step at a Time: Ceridian's Story

When sales and profits start to fall, a CEO's knee-jerk reaction may be to push his people harder to achieve results. While this tactic may work in the short term, it is detrimental to the long-term success of an organization. It breeds low engagement, high turnover, and a lack of trust in the future sustainability of a company. Instead, skilled CEOs diagnose the foundational problems in their business, treat the cause instead of the symptom, and ultimately bring balance between purpose and execution to the organization.

Bringing such balance requires nine deliberate steps:

1. Defining organizational purpose
2. Understanding the need for change
3. Enhancing communication
4. Painting a clear vision

5. Aligning of values
6. Placing the right people in the right roles
7. Connecting mission
8. Measuring outcomes
9. Acting with intention

One CEO who effectively brought balance, accelerated people engagement, and increased business results to his organization by employing these steps is David Ossip, one of the highest rated CEOs on Glassdoor's Employees' Choice Awards list.[1] When he took over as CEO of the global human capital management technology company Ceridian a little more than three years ago, he inherited a heavily unbalanced organization with a highly disengaged workforce, a Glassdoor rating below 2, and declining business results.

"My take home after a hard look at Ceridian was that the organization had to reinvent its culture in order to drive proper employee engagement, in turn improving our customer engagement scores and market share," Ossip recalls.

Ossip considers himself an entrepreneur at heart, not a corporate executive. He has a successful track record of building start-ups in the human resources space. He met the Ceridian organization shortly after he started his last company, Dayforce, in 2009. Dayforce owned strong workforce management technology for scheduling, planning, and tracking employees. Ceridian's large market presence and great reputation in services placed it at the top of its industry, but it lacked strong innovation and technology. With no new products in its pipeline, it lost market share. The combination hurt both people engagement and customer satisfaction scores—two key metrics that can make or break the success of an organization.

"When I saw Ceridian, I saw a good opportunity to create something special by taking world-class software and pairing it with an established organization that had no new-product pipeline," Ossip recalls. A partnership was formed in 2011 with a relaunch of Dayforce under Ceridian's brand. "We had forecasted 100 customer purchases and ended up selling 483," Ossip recalls proudly.

The following year, a market survey determined the industry pain points. The survey highlighted that HR professionals were frustrated by the lack of integration and communication between HR computer applications. None of the systems spoke to one another, and it made the HR practitioners' day-to-day work difficult because it slowed down and limited business outcomes. The solution: extend the Dayforce technology into the payroll, benefits, and other talent management modules so the entire employee experience could be captured and tracked through one application. The market expressed strong interest in the solution, but the move only made sense from an execution standpoint if Ceridian were to acquire Dayforce. Ossip accepted the role of CEO of Ceridian once the merger was complete.

Ossip's first executive meeting yielded one key consensus: without high people engagement, Ceridian could not drive the other changes it wanted and required. People engagement had to become the organization's core focus.

Ossip, his team, and Ceridian embarked on a disciplined approach designed to turn the company around. Ceridian, founded in 1932, had a strong history of execution but forgot why it existed in the first place—its purpose—and the values that drove the business. Plus, not much of the original culture at Ceridian had evolved beyond 1960.

1. Defining Organizational Purpose

Ceridian had established a trusted brand around delivering results but realized this definition was vague and lacked focus regarding why the organization was started in the first place. Ossip, his team, and ultimately the organization came to the conclusion that their core purpose centered around improving work and life for people—employees and customers alike.

"Our worldwide focus became something more than just paying people correctly," Ossip explains. "For anyone who was a customer, whether you were an employee, a manager, a CEO, or a COO, work and life would be improved by our software and our services."

In addition, Ceridian sold off businesses unrelated to its established core purpose. It focused its assets in human capital management.

2. Understanding the Need for Change

Ceridian originated as part of IBM. Due to antitrust laws, the unit was spun out and acquired by Control Data Corporation. In 1993, the company was transformed into Ceridian by the then-CEO. "I think at the time he wanted to create a legacy," Ossip says. The company was highly diversified and profitable but lacked focus. It resembled an old bank—barriers halted communication and promoted a more rigid method of planning and decision making, all without the feedback of its people. The structures of the company prevented change instead of driving it.

"If you have an organization that can't change, you will become extinct," Ossip insists.

3. Enhancing Communication

"The existing methods of communication were a constraint rather than an enabler. People had great ideas but no way to communicate to the leaders of the organization, and the leaders did not really seem interested in listening anyway. Ceridian was stuck in the 1960s when it came to its internal processes," Ossip shares.

The barriers to communication were not only cultural but physical, too.

"In fact, the first time I went into the main office in Minneapolis," Ossip says, "I wasn't even sure I'd be let into the office based on what I was wearing. I showed up to find large, flat screens in a beautiful lobby boldly warning those entering of the dress code." His attire: jeans and a casual shirt.

Ossip recalls uncomfortably entering the "executive floor," where traditional physical structures had leaders sequestered in their offices and administration staff positioned between them and all other people. Regardless of intent, these structures promoted an "us and them" mindset.

"I sort of scratched my head and said, 'No, this cannot work in today's environment,'" Ossip explains. He started to think of the processes and programs that promote more open and regular communications.

Among other things, Ceridian instituted a program called Top Talent to improve people–leadership interaction. Under this initiative, people working at the company proposed improvement ideas. The ideas were judged by a team of Ceridian senior leaders. The top five selections were funded, implemented, and celebrated.

Another change involved coaching existing leaders on effective communication. New leaders were interviewed on their ability to effectively communicate and manage change, which communicated the organization's commitment to evolution. Also, the "executive floor" no longer exists.

4. Painting a Clear Vision

"For me, the ultimate goal of Ceridian is to become the preferred HR solution chosen by the employee. In other words, if someone is interviewing at a particular company, they ask if Dayforce is used at the organization because they know it will make their work and life better," Ossip says. He rallied the organization behind this vision, painting a picture for his people of what the company's future would look like if they got it right. The message transformed the organization's energy for the monumental task at hand.

5. Aligning Values

An employee survey revealed that people knew what the company values were but did not identify with them. Nor did they believe the organization was living these values. With a clear purpose defined, values that would support and drive the business could be adopted. Ossip noted:

> The first value we chose was around customer focus, which for us was the concept of listening carefully to our customers and acting with empathy toward them.
>
> Second, we spoke about transparency—open communication, maintaining a high degree of integrity, and making sure we were accountable for our behaviors.
>
> Third, diligence and optimism. The belief was that you had to be optimistic in order to succeed. That optimism is a planned behavior, meaning it starts with proper preparation and diligence. That preparation leads to knowledge, and that knowledge leads to confidence. In turn, confidence drives success. The entire concept was that if you do the proper prep and diligence you will be successful and you should be optimistic.
>
> The last thing we spoke about was agility. By acting as agile individuals we would be prepared and enthused to see new challenges. We knew with proper preparation and diligence that we would achieve success.

Ossip and his team then ensured an effective program was in place to communicate the new values and to ensure that people were living and demonstrating them. They created and distributed a book called *Our Way—a* series of internal and external case studies showing how the company's purpose and values drove success and how living those values transformed work and life for the better.

Eighteen-inch letters declaring Ceridian's new values were plastered on the walls throughout the building. Their purpose was not to impress but to remind people of these expectations. Company values are reinforced at the start of every meeting and discussed on an ongoing basis. Ceridian's values are now part of the cultural DNA that drives the organization's purpose. "The values instilled by David and our leaders have really permeated the workplace," Deepak Abrol, a sales solutions consultant shares. "It makes it feel like I'm working with people who are all here for the same reasons. Because we're all on the same page I feel comfortable bringing anyone else in the company in on a sales call or demo."

6. Placing the Right People in the Right Roles

Ossip recalls recruiting for a previous start-up of his: "We grew from $0 to $100 million in three years. We kept hiring until we hit one hundred people. We then looked around and thought, 'Who have we hired? How do we use their talents to accomplish our goals? Do we have the right people to achieve success?' We had no process in place to answer these questions." Ossip learned the hard way that recruiting is more than just filling seats in an organization. It requires ensuring that the right people, who can drive your purpose forward, fill the right roles.

"We then had to make a lot of tough decisions to move people to new roles, and even remove people who weren't aligned with what we needed to do. We basically had to restructure and rebuild the organization," Ossip says.

Ossip retained this knowledge from past experiences and utilized it to improve Ceridian. "We typically have candidates meet with about five different people in the company—some who they will be working with and others outside of their department," he says. First and foremost, Ceridian looks for a purpose and culture "FIT." These are people who believe in what Ceridian is attempting to do, who like to have **F**un, are **I**ntelligent, and will work well with others in **T**eams.

If you flew from Yorkshire, England, to California in the United States with a coworker, would you sit in the seat next to him or would you escape to the back of the plane and avoid him? "We want people who want to sit with each other," Ossip explains. "When it comes to intelligence, we test not if the person knows everything at the time of the hire, but whether or not the person has the ability and aptitude to learn. We also want people who are more interested in a team than a specific title or role." What people do best plays heavily into a placement decision, too. Ceridian's goal is to have its people playing to their strengths as much as possible.

Under Ossip's direction, Ceridian's interview process now includes examining backgrounds and resumes, assessing a candidate's strengths, and testing for FIT, core communication, and convictions. The process is now geared to examining relatability of the potential person to his hiring manager, team, and peers.

"If employee engagement and productivity improve, and attrition drops, we know we are getting it right," Ossip adds.

7. Connecting Mission

Ossip and his team further defined Ceridian's mission to ensure everyone knew what they needed to do to remain in line with the company's stated purpose and values. They are now "creating products and services that will help people enjoy work and life more."

8. Measuring Outcomes

Ceridian implements an anonymous people engagement survey twice a year with results broken down to the department and team level. It also uses a daily people engagement tool built into the Dayforce product. "We get the results and we communicate them back to the employees and the managers completely openly. We let both the good and the bad out," Ossip relates.

Ceridian's key measurement is how internal people engagement tracks to customer service experience scores. "We identify the top five areas of organizational improvement and we put in programs to treat those five items. We report back to the employees as to our progress against those initiatives, and then we survey again," Ossip explains.

Ceridian not only looks for triggers of engagement but triggers of disengagement, too. Triggers of disengagement can be small things. They might be a time-consuming expense process, a poor travel or time-off policy, a mandatory dress code, outdated tools or systems, or the way attendance is monitored. Often, these triggers are the small things that you don't hear about but that upset people.

Disengagement triggers cause people to disconnect from the workplace. When this happens, they shift to a nine-to-five mentality, performance drops, customer satisfaction declines, and the company starts missing targets. Organizations with many of these disengagement triggers often struggle to get the type of people commitment they need to drive engagement, execution, and business results.

Ossip hosts regular town halls and walkarounds to meet with people in an open forum and listen to their concerns. This is the best way to learn what is going on before it becomes a problem.

"Whether it be revenue, ACV [annual contract value in terms of sales], client retention, or employee attrition, when employee engagement goes down, they all go bad; when engagement goes up, they all improve," Ossip reports.

9. Acting with Intention

Ceridian regularly surveys its people not only about their engagement but also concerning their understanding and connection to company values. This includes how well people and leaders are living the organization's values. People, managers, and teams then identify the areas of improvement required and take action to make enhancements. They also celebrate outcomes. Acting with intention was the most critical part of Ossip's successful change management.

One example he cites is Ceridian's Dayforce app launch in 2012. The company sold more than twenty-eight hundred systems in three years. The biggest constraint with that volume involved implementation. The organization ramped up its implementation team from one hundred team members to one thousand people in a three-year period.

In order to allow implementation to keep pace with sales, Ceridian increased the project load for many of its consultants. The decision yielded a revenue increase but also a decline in people engagement and retention. Indicators warned that revenue would slow if Ceridian didn't make additional changes to remedy the added strain on its people. Based on feedback from its people, the company adjusted resources within the workload. In a very short time, people engagement rose again.

Ceridian's effective actions resulted in a record-breaking two hundred new accounts in one month.

The lesson here is that if you continually listen to your people, seek their feedback, and act on valid concerns, you can avoid bad business outcomes. If you let people engagement issues continue unchecked, the negativity will quickly spread throughout your organization and damage your business.

Ceridian's annual planning process for each upcoming year starts early in the third quarter. Planning covers not only financials but also the underpinnings of what allows the organization to hit its numbers—people and customer engagement.

"A good portion of our planning and budgeting process involves conversations around people metrics, things like our employee engagement year-over-year, our Net Promoter scores concerning our customer engagement, and conversations about important topics like attrition," Ossip says.

On a monthly basis, Ceridian reports on progress to top managers in the company, and they in turn share the information with their people. On a quarterly basis, Ossip shares company results openly with all employees. "We have a company all-hands call where I present for 25 percent of the time and take questions for the remainder of the meeting," Ossip explains. All questions are responded to, regardless of how challenging they may be.

On the people engagement survey side, Ceridian reports to the managers and employees all the way down to department or team level. Everything is open and shared. When executives discover low engagement, the organization looks at the whole business area with an extra focus on the person managing the team. Based on feedback from its people, Ceridian makes changes not only in the way the company is run but also who runs it.

"You know you've got an engaged workforce when you walk through the halls and there's a buzz—a sense of positive energy inside the office. I contrast this to the first time I walked into the office in Minneapolis. It was like walking into a dark museum," Ossip recalls. When he held his first town hall meetings, no one asked questions. Nowadays, the meetings run over because energized people ask questions and give feedback. People report that there is an open, honest, and trusted environment at Ceridian. This environment has bred more than just engaged people; it has also impressively accelerated business outcomes.

Over the following eighteen months of Ossip's change management initiative, people engagement scores rose significantly, and Ceridian's Glassdoor rating went from less than 2 to higher than 4 on a scale of 1 to 5. Furthermore, customer satisfaction as measured by the industry's Net Promoter scores increased a record 25 points year over year. On the revenue side, Ceridian's Dayforce flagship product saw a 70 percent growth rate year over year, and the organization became one of the fastest growing cloud companies in the marketplace.

"In addition, employee attrition went down, customer retention went up, and our business began to thrive. The inflection point was changing the model of how we engage employees. Employee experience is our number-one goal. The second is customer experience, and third is product excellence," Ossip concludes. Ceridian was one of Canada's Top 100 Employers for 2016.[2]

Ossip's vision and direction clearly brought needed change and outcomes to Ceridian. The company's success lies in a balance of understanding the organization's purpose and executing on needed business deliverables to fulfill that purpose.

Striking a Balance at Humana

The rising cost of health care is one of the most pressing problems facing American society. According to the Centers for Disease Control and

Prevention (CDC), 86 percent of health-care costs are incurred due to chronic diseases.[3] These are diseases that in many cases can be prevented and mitigated by changes in lifestyle and access to preventive care. By taking simple steps like ensuring people have access to healthy food, a safe place to exercise, and a place to engage with preventive care providers, the health-care system can make a significant impact on the health of communities—and reduce health-care costs.

As part of Humana's commitment to reducing health-care costs, the company created a Bold Goal[4] to improve the health of the communities it serves by 20 percent by the year 2020. Humana is tracking its progress by using the Healthy Days Measurement developed by the CDC. This measurement asks four simple questions about how respondents feel physically and mentally and has proven to align closely with other clinical measures of population health.

"We have placed the Bold Goal at the center of our business. Not only has the Bold Goal aligned strategy and tactics across the company, it has also shifted our business model and placed it in the context of making society better," Bruce Broussard, CEO of Humana, says. Like National Life, Humana's focus is to do well by doing good. "By improving the health of the population, we can also lower costs," Broussard adds.

"Our Bold Goal has also given our company a deeper purpose. Along with our values, it has improved the engagement of our employees, enabling them to connect their day-to-day work to a higher cause," Broussard explains. Humana has seen the impact of this in a number of ways, such as through a significant increase in employees volunteering their time to organizations that are helping to improve community health. It has also accelerated a more customer-centric culture. Broussard concludes:

> We cannot achieve our goal without the engagement of our customers. Health is personal, and engagement requires trust. Building trust with our customers is something we must do every day—by simplifying and personalizing their experience. We are passionate about this and have accelerated our investments and innovations in

> areas that enable us to create this kind of experience. Personalizing our approach with our customers is about finding those moments of influence where we can positively impact someone's health—in the end, that's what is most important.

Health care is local. Each community has its own unique barriers to health, and each community also has a unique health-care ecosystem. These must be addressed to improve health. That's why a critical component of Humana's strategy has been to engage and partner with for-profit and nonprofit entities in the community. The company has been successful in establishing a strategy that it has rolled out to several communities, which includes a collaborative group of organizations dedicated to improving the health of the community and the health of those who live in it.

"Part of this approach involves replacing the decades-old fee-for-service model for physician reimbursement, which pays doctors for each procedure performed, with an accountable care model that rewards doctors for improving the health outcomes of their patients.[5] Preventive and proactive, this approach represents our new purpose put into action," Broussard explains.

The Bold Goal has already made measurable strides in improving the health of Humana's employees. That's because 20 percent health improvement for them has an earlier timetable—by 2017. Between 2012 and 2015, four out of ten associates had decreased their number of health risks closely linked to the development of chronic disease and another three out of ten had sustained or improved their fitness levels.[6]

By focusing on "doing good" in a way that is aligned with Humana's business model, the company has created a highly engaged workforce with a deep alignment to the business's strategy and tactics. Through lowered costs, it has also increased the number of Healthy Days in the communities they serve and grown its health plan membership.

"And this is only the beginning," Broussard says.

Chapter Questions

As this chapter deals with getting the balance between purpose and execution right in your organization, the following questions should be used as a check-list to ensure that your organization has all the components in place to ensure balance, accelerated people engagement, and enhanced business results.

These questions should be asked and answered by you and others in the organization.

Organizational Purpose

- Do I and others know and believe in our organization's purpose?

Communication

- Has my organization's purpose and any need for change been clearly communicated and understood by people working in the business?

Vision

- Do I and others see and believe where our organization is going?
- Do I and others believe the work we do each day is helping us drive in that direction?

Values

- Do I and others know, believe in, and live the values of our organization?
- If so, do our values support the fulfillment of our purpose and vision?

Right People/Right Roles

- Do I and others in my organization play to our strengths nearly 80 percent of the time?

Mission

- Do I and others see the connection of our daily work to fulfilling our organization's purpose and vision?

Measurement

- Is there a mechanism in place to ask and receive regular feedback from people working within my business and from our customers?
- If so, do people feel comfortable giving this feedback, and do they feel it is valued?
- Does my organization measure its balance between purpose and execution, internal and external people engagement, and correlated business outcomes?

Action

- Does my organization take swift action when change is needed?
- If so, are these consistently the right actions to overcome challenges and seize opportunities?
- Are successful actions shared and celebrated?

Notes

1. "Employees' Choice Awards Highest Rated CEOs." https://www.glassdoor.ca/Award/Highest-Rated-CEOs-Canada-LST_KQ0,25.htm?utm_medium=email&utm_source=newsletter&utm_campaign=June2016_CA&utm_content=HighestRatedCEO_CA16.
2. Richard Yerema and Kristina Leung. "Recognized as One of Canada's Top 100 Employers (2016)." November 8, 2015. http://content.eluta.ca/top-employer-ceridian.
3. "Chronic Disease Prevention and Health Promotion." *Center for Disease Control*. www.cdc.gov/chronicdisease/.
4. "Humana 2020: Our Commitment to Serve." https://closethegap.humana.com/2020goal/.
5. "Accountable Care at Humana." https://www.humana.com/provider/support/accountable-care/.
6. "Humana 2020 2015 Progress Report." https://closethegap.humana.com/reports/Humana-2020-Progress-Report.pdf.

CHAPTER 12

Changing the World Through Leadership

Be the change that you wish to see in the world.

—Mahatma Gandhi

You do not need to aspire to be Gandhi, Mother Teresa, or Nelson Mandela to change your organization or the world for the better. However, like these transformational leaders, you must lead by example and sincerely want to add value to others. It must be an active choice. An organization is an extension of the behaviors of its leaders. If you want to change your organization, change the way you lead first.

Creating Social and Economic Value

Starbucks' purpose is to share great coffee with friends and make the world better.

Despite not being a coffee drinker myself, I have spent a significant amount of time at Starbucks cafés around the world. I have written (even some of this book), worked, had meetings, and met friends and family there. In addition, I have satisfied my wife's cravings for a good cup of tea and my eight-year-old's brownie request or four-year-old's banana nut bread fix on weekend outings. Starbucks has been a big part of my life for the past fifteen years, both personally and professionally.

Scott Pitasky, the executive vice president and chief partner resources officer for the global partner resources organization (human resources) of Starbucks, once asked me if I had ever had a bad experience at Starbucks in order to help me understand the secret to the company's people engagement efforts. I thought about it for split second and then confidently said, "No." With what must have been hundreds of visits and even more transactions on my end at various locations around the world, this is more than impressive. Surely, I would have run across at least one employee somewhere in my travels who was having a bad day—but honestly, no, I have not a single bad experience that I can recall.

"Why is this?" I asked Pitasky. His response was:

> We sincerely care for our partners [people who work at Starbucks] and they in turn care for our customers. We have always known that the more engaged our partners are, the more engaged our customers are. We have a pretty good culture of our people holding us accountable for what we stand for. Our greatest strengths are the commitment and pride of our people. This stems from a heritage of investing in them and sharing in our success.

Pitasky believes that organizations that will thrive and lead in the future are the ones that figure out how to effectively invest in creating both social and economic value. He characterizes the efforts of Starbucks to achieve this goal with a cake metaphor.

Pitasky describes organizations where he worked in the past that ran their business and generated profits. They gave back through employee giving, disaster relief, and community involvement. But this was just the icing on the cake. The goal of creating social and economic value, according to Pitasky, is to turn what in some organizations is just the icing on the cake into the cake itself. "This is done through prioritizing and being true to your organizational purpose. It not only creates success, but it also makes your business stronger. Icing only takes you so far," Pitasky explains.

Starbucks recently made a commitment to hiring ten thousand veterans and military spouses. It also provides, in partnership with Arizona State University, an opportunity for partners to earn their bachelor's degree with full tuition coverage through the company's College Achievement Program. "The people who come out of this program tend to be some of our most talented and committed partners," Pitasky says.

Both of these programs—and many others—show how Starbucks is striving to invest in creating social and economic value. Its hiring efforts add social value by tapping into and employing highly talented people who are simply overlooked in the job market. This practice creates economic value through employment, consumer spending, and for Starbucks itself.

In addition to Starbucks' commitment to investing in a diversified workforce and the education of its people, the company champions the same care with its coffee growers and suppliers around the world. The "Starbucks Supplier Social Responsibility Standards: Manufactured Goods and Services" policy states:

> Starbucks endeavors to work with businesses that train and develop their employees, and that work with governments and communities in which they operate to improve the educational, environmental, cultural, economic, and social well-being of those communities.[1]

For more than fifteen years, Starbucks has partnered with Conservation International, a not-for-profit global environmental protection organization, to work toward its commitment to 100 percent ethical sourcing of its coffee around the world. That means sourcing that is sustainable, transparent, and good for people and the planet. Covering four continents, its partnership has improved the lives of more than one million farmers and workers around the world. Starbucks is leading the industry by currently ethically sourcing 99 percent of its coffee.[2]

Another example of Starbucks' leadership in creating social and economic value is its work with the Eastern Congo Initiative, a charity organization founded by Ben Affleck to advocate for and secure grants to improve the lives of people in eastern Congo. Through this partnership, Starbucks has helped thousands of struggling coffee farmers in the Democratic Republic of Congo to increase their production, creating jobs and opportunity in local communities.

While Starbucks has led significant positive social and economic contributions since it opened its doors in 1971, it still sees itself in the early stages of creating real value for the world. "There is much work to do to find balance between performance and conscience for Starbucks and other public companies," Pitasky says.

One organization that Pitasky admires for its commitment to sustainability is Patagonia, the outdoor clothing retailer. When you navigate to the company's website, clothing is not the first thing you see. Instead, you first land on a home page that reads, "Vote Our Planet. Defend Our Air, Our Water, Our Soil." In fact, at first glance, the organization looks more like an environmental advocacy group than a retail company. Even American photographer and environmentalist Ansel Adams is featured on the site with the quote, "It is horrifying that we have to fight our own government to save the environment."

Patagonia's mission statement is, "Build the best product, cause no unnecessary harm, use business to inspire and implement solutions to the environmental crisis." Its mission is fueled by its business success. Its business success is fueled by its mission. The organization's focus on environmental and social responsibility is unmistakable. Like Starbucks, Patagonia is balancing its purpose and execution to help make the world a better place.

According to Pitasky, the core behind achieving a culture that contributes social and economic value is the level of organizational commitment behind it. Pitasky spoke of a "wave of change" coming that will require both a social and economic transformation. Companies that get this and get on board will thrive in the future. Companies that don't will struggle. "There is a bit of a perfect storm of change," Pitasky says. "Millennials and society at large care about this, and organizations must get it right to compete for customers and the best talent."

What Pitasky is talking about is a powerful concept that impacts every part of a business and its leadership. The three core attributes for such a culture are trust, belief, and pride in what you are doing. The workforce today is fluid and requires organizations to create a culture that retains the best talent and ensures a commitment to the organization.

"It is about looking under the hood of your organization," Pitasky explains. "An established purpose, vision, mission, and values must be there. Also, how much they really matter to the organization is important. Every business and leader must have a North Star that guides him or her every day. They must be committed to living up to it. There must be a differentiator that is bigger and more important than just profits and shareholder value. This is what high-performing organizations and truly great servant leaders understand. The outcome of what you do creates shareholder value, not the other way around."

The bigger you get as an organization, the more deliberate you need to be in creating cultural tenets that matter to your people, customers, and communities. The language and taxonomy you use and the way leaders communicate it are critical.

Pitasky compares an organizational culture to a plant. If the organization is deeply rooted in its values and purpose, it doesn't waver when things become difficult. The organization stays true to the values it holds. The cultural tenets remain important because they are embedded deeply within the foundation and leadership of the organization. What it stands for is its default.

"The best way to know you're on the right path to creating social and economic value is to look at the narrative of your company. If you take all the external comments about your organization over a six-month period and put them together, what will the narrative say? How does it compare to what your internal people say? Most importantly, do both describe who you are and what you want and need to be? If not, you have a problem," Pitasky suggests.

What Pitasky is referring to is your organization's reputation—your brand. It's an accumulation of all that drives your internal and external engagement—ultimately, the way you lead as an organization, both inside and out.

Starbucks has been able to accelerate people engagement and drive business outcomes through a strong leadership commitment to its purpose, values, and executional excellences. Today, the coffee house has more than twenty-four thousand locations worldwide, with many more likely to come. This enables the organization to rapidly expand the social and economic value it is creating for the world. Everything Starbucks does is through the leadership lens of humanity.

Practicing Servant Leadership

According to Pitasky, the essential foundation of creating a culture that drives social and economic value requires embracing servant leadership. Starbucks' culture cannot exist without it. The ability for leaders to be humble and vulnerable is critically important.

Based on my two decades of work with leaders and leadership teams in diverse industries around the world, both big and small, good and bad, I agree with Pitasky. After intently studying the behaviors and business results of the leaders I worked with over the years, the common denominator for success is clear: servant leadership—putting their people first in all cases.[3]

Deloitte partner Jennifer Knickerbocker asserts that leadership is "all about putting people first and understanding that your success is directly linked to the success of those you lead. If you believe that your success is linked to theirs, enabling the success of those you lead is a natural priority. When you invest in people in a way that makes them perform better, you'll be better for it too, and the results you achieve together will be greater. Doing these things leads to a higher sense of engagement, performance, retention, and communication." Knickerbocker has been instrumental in orchestrating more than $100 million in pro bono services for organizations, including Girl Scouts, Dress for Success, and YWCA.

Servant leadership has been a staple of every corporate and leadership talk I have given for more than a decade. Unfortunately, many corporate structures are not set up to encourage or foster selfless behavior. Nor does acting with a sense of altruism toward others come naturally to every leader. In fact, in most cases, personal leadership objectives fail to recognize or reward the successful development and growth of others.

In *People Follow You: The Real Secret to What Matters Most in Leadership*, Jeb Blount explains: "Ultimately, people follow leaders they like, trust, and believe in, leading to higher productivity and long-term development. Managers don't get paid for what they do but rather for the performance of their people. By putting people first, you'll position yourself and your company for success."[4]

Dan Price is the CEO of Seattle, Washington–based Gravity Payments, a credit card processing company serving more than ten thousand clients nationally. Its motto: "The only way to do business is to serve others, do more for them, and charge less." The company's career page offers unlimited paid time off, Flannel Fridays, and the cultural statement, "Take care of your employees, and they'll take care of your customers." It was awarded Washington's Best Workplaces award.[5]

In an extreme and controversial example of servant leadership, Price reduced his own compensation from about $1 million annually to $70,000 in order to subsidize wage increases for his workers.

Knowing the challenges his lower-wage workers faced buying homes or making ends meet, Price instituted a new minimum wage at his company, setting all employees to a salary of at least $70,000 per year.[6] Many employees doubled their salaries, which altered their lives for the better.[7]

"If we're actually able to pay everybody enough that they can live a normal life, within a mile or two of our office, then to me, there is a moral imperative to create some standard, some [salary] floor," Price says.

Despite the initial naysayers and admittedly bumpy and challenging road after implementation of the policy, Price's initiative brought a flood of new clients and job applicants who supported his social responsibility.

In a show of appreciation, Price's employees surprised him with a gift of a Tesla Model S.[8]

Servant leaders put the needs of others before their own. This includes their employees, customers, families, and communities. They believe that serving others is their mission in life. They count their successes by the number of times they are able to help others thrive.

Robert Greenleaf, the renowned leadership development expert and father of the term "servant leadership," felt the heart of the concept is captured in the assertion, "My success is your success." He went on to say that "Servant-leaders differ from other persons of goodwill because they act on what they believe."[9] To describe how you can excel as a servant leader, Greenleaf outlined the "10 Leadership Characteristics" critical to success:

Listening: a deep commitment to honestly listen to others
Empathy: a striving to understand and empathize with others
Healing: the potential for healing one's self and one's relationship to others
Awareness: a keen awareness of their surroundings and self
Persuasion: an ability to convince others and build consensus
Conceptualization: the ability to think short- and long-term and pursue "impossible" dreams
Foresight: a drive to reflect on the lessons of the past, embrace the realities of the present, and envision the likely consequences of a decision for the future
Stewardship: a sincere and emotional commitment to care for things important to others
Commitment to the growth of people: a focus on helping others become better people—professionally and personally
Building community: the ability to pull people together for a greater good[10]

In life, the more you serve others, the more success and fulfillment you will enjoy. It is a basic truth of humanity. The same holds true for leadership.

As an individual contributor, you perform the work yourself. When you lead people, you must shift your focus to ensuring that others can perform their work successfully. To do this effectively, your role must shift to serving your people and teams, not the other way around.

In the article "The Advantages of the Servant Leadership Style," author George N. Root III states, "Leaders that use the servant leadership style tend to gain a great deal of respect and trust from their employees, according to psychology professor Paul T. P. Wong of Tyndale University College in Toronto. The strong positive feelings between management and employees that the servant leadership style promotes translate into a high sense of morale. When employees are satisfied with their jobs and their company, workplace productivity rises."

The success of embracing a leadership style and organizational culture that practices servant leadership has its roots in religious institutions, educational systems, and the military. It fosters high people engagement and delivers winning business results. Employing and developing foundational leaders with this leadership model in mind supports and creates lasting and successful organizations.

History has proven that the more you serve others in life, the more abundance shows up in your own life. Plus, studies and reports show that, "when we make the effort to give without expectations of reciprocity, we feel fulfilled and energized."[11] As organizations like Starbucks, Greyston Bakery, Gravity Payments, and other great companies and institutions written about in this book demonstrate, servant leadership is a powerful force for effective leadership, business outcomes, and positive social change.

Leadership Lessons from the Littlest Green Beret

Jan Rutherford is a former U.S. Army Special Forces soldier, twenty-five-year business executive, senior instructor at the University of

Colorado Denver Business School, speaker, strategist, coach, and author of *The Littlest Green Beret: On Self-Reliant Leadership*. In 2011, he founded the leadership development firm Self-Reliant Leadership, LLC.

Rutherford entered the U.S. Army at age seventeen (weighing only 114 pounds), and spent six years in Special Forces as a medic and "A" team executive officer and three years as a military intelligence officer. He is an expert on overcoming challenges to strengthen resilience and lead more effectively. He believes the best way to grow an organization is by developing the people within it.

Rutherford frequently has CEOs tell him that their goal is to grow their business 10 percent or so. His response is always, "Tell me what that means to the people on your team."

A top- or bottom-line growth number doesn't translate for most people doing the work in an organization. "As a leader, you must put your goals in language people can execute on," Rutherford says. People need to know what they need to accomplish each day in line with the organization's larger purpose. Growing a business by a certain monetary amount means very little to most people, who certainly don't get out of bed each morning for P&L improvements. Statements and direction that create alignment between the organization's purpose and what people execute on each day must be a CEO's focus.

"Special Operations soldiers want and need to understand the commander's intent. The why. What is the purpose of what we're trying to accomplish?" Rutherford explains. "In the military, this gets translated down to a five-paragraph operations order. At every level of that operations order it gets more detailed." In a corporate setting, this is equivalent to what is called V2MOM at Salesforce.com: Vision, Values, Methods, Obstacles, and Metrics. Needed actions are clarified for people working for the organization from a high-level purpose down to the nitty-gritty execution.

"As a former CEO, I wanted to create shared accountability so that I didn't have to micromanage," Rutherford says. As a leader, inspiring people to a purpose and vision is in some ways the easy part. The hard part is getting people to truly commit. When you have shared accountability, people do what they commit to, which is actually keeping the promises they made to the team and one another. There are consequences for meeting and exceeding standards. There should also be consequences for letting the team down.

"People don't die for their country—they die for their buddy," Rutherford affirms. It goes back to getting someone to buy into an organization's purpose. At some point it becomes about shared accountability, peers, and being truly selfless.

"It's all about connections, relationships, and people," Rutherford explains. "I think curiosity is the prerequisite of genuinely caring for other people, which is the prerequisite of actively listening to others. It's only then that you can hope to inspire the confidence in people to commit—in a disciplined fashion—along with the personal sacrifices that lead to focus and performance."

Leadership on the Front Lines

"It starts with core values. If you're not a passionate, committed, and enthusiastic leader—if you are not emulating characteristics of honor, integrity, and courage, your team will not do so either," fighter pilot Waldo Waldman says.

People need to see their leaders leading by example before they start to behave the same way. Waldman calls it "emulating excellence." "Often, people fight for their leader more than they fight for the mission." What they see in their leader inspires them to action and greatness.

When Waldman was living in tents in Iraq, Saudi Arabia, and the Republic of South Korea and his squadron was getting ready to fly and get shot at, it was the bond that his commanders created that made the difference. "The camaraderie, community, and brotherhood we had overruled the stress and fear that was so omnipresent," Waldman says. "It starts and sometimes ends with the commander. Senior leaders must keep the passion for what you want and need to achieve, connect with the troops, and emulate excellence every single day."

Waldman explains, "It's the human component, the inspiration, the encouragement, and the caring that goes so far above and beyond the mission and purpose of a fighter squadron. Once you feel your commander cares about you, once he knows about your mission and values and really wants to help you accomplish them, you'll be more loyal to him. You'll volunteer for the tough duties, you'll study more, practice more, because you don't want to let him down. And when you become better, the whole squadron becomes better and performance keeps improving one person at a time."

Waldman says you need to be two things as a leader: approachable and coachable. "If someone sees a target or threat to me I want him or her to call it out to me," Waldman explains. This applies to his time in the Air Force and currently in his business. If there is a missile heading in your direction, you want to know about it. If you are not approachable, you will be caught off guard in all situations. If you are not coachable, you won't adapt to new environments and circumstances as needed.

"I think leaders should be coachable and willing to change. If you love what you do and are passionate about it, you've got to be able to humble yourself and seek coaching to continuously improve your execution and get better. This is about being able to ask for help and being approachable to others for the same reason. Complacency kills—as a fighter pilot and a businessperson," Waldman concludes.

Fostering Transparency

Building a culture around purpose and executional excellence requires transparency as a leader and organization. People need to see their leaders in action doing what they expect of them—being sincere, genuine, and honest to themselves and others. Delivering lip service to an idea, being overly secretive, or being disingenuous is an engagement and loyalty killer.

"Don't give the CEO speech, live what you are talking about and show up every day in that manner. It starts with you," Mehran Assadi of National Life Group explains. He adds:

> I'm talking to you from my office, which sits in the middle of the marketing distribution and product area. There are no walls, it's all glass. Everyone sees what I do. Everyone sees what's on my board. Ninety percent of my meetings are in this space. In the past, a lot of people would say there's a lot of confidential stuff that happens with a CEO and that other people shouldn't necessarily see who's going in and out of his or her office. But that's bull. At some point, people get tired of watching who's coming and going. People begin to realize that there are no organized patterns behind any of it. When it becomes normal, there's nothing exciting to see anymore.

Transparency in leadership and the organization feeds trust. When people are kept in the dark, they tend to spend valuable time making assumptions. In most cases, these assumptions are inaccurate and foster false rumors. When transparency and trust are high, the people focus is on important business tasks at hand.

Evolution, Not Revolution

From the time I was a kid, I have been a motivational speech junkie. I love them. While I'm running, I will listen to everything from Jesse Jackson to Tony Robbins. As they are designed to do, these speeches motivate and inspire me. One powerful story that has had quite a bit of play on the motivational speech circuit is the Bamboo Story.

The Bamboo Story basically recounts the growth cycle of a Chinese Bamboo tree.[12] Once the tree is planted, it needs up to five years of watering, care, and nurturing before it breaks ground. But once it does, it can grow up to ninety feet in five weeks. Quite amazing!

The moral of the story is that persistence and dedication pay off.

I recently read another take on the Bamboo Story by Noah St. John in his *Early to Rise* blog, entitled "Why I Hate the Bamboo Story."[13] In the blog post, St. John criticizes the story's message, saying that successful people don't continue to do things over and over again without seeing a result. This is true, and I agree with him. However, if you are growing a Chinese Bamboo tree, you know something is happening below the Earth's surface that you can't see. You have faith, trust, and knowledge that your efforts and actions will produce a grand tree when the work is done and the time is right.

Unfortunately, most corporate leadership is wired for short-term thinking. Few will ever see the bamboo tree because if they can't see immediate results, they turn elsewhere. Despite this, some of the most celebrated successes in history have been a result of building something below the surface—with no visual signs of the outcome—before it skyrockets. Henry Ford had five business failures before he succeeded with Ford Motor Company. Richard Hooker's comedy war novel *M*A*S*H* took seven years and twenty-one publisher rejections before it became a best seller, movie, and the longest-running television series of all time. Horse jockey Eddie Arcaro lost 250 races before going on to win seventeen Triple Crowns and 554 stake races with total earnings of more than $30 million. And the Beatles performed about twelve hundred times—sometimes in strip clubs—before they broke out.[14]

No corporate culture will change overnight. The correct actions you put in place today will evolve your organization to where it needs to be in the future. Culture change is evolution, not revolution. And in the most sustainable cases, this process is slow but steady. Inasmuch as Purpose Meets Execution is a cultural change initiative, the same principle applies. While quick wins will be available as you address low-hanging fruit in your business, you will need time, persistence, and consistency of leadership to fully embed a mindset of purpose and execution into your organizational foundation and realize its maximum value. Once you arrive, people engagement and business results will accelerate like a bamboo shoot.

The Power of Storytelling

One of the most powerful cultural change tools leaders have is storytelling. Not only will it help bring organizational purpose to life, as illustrated earlier in this book, but it also brings credibility, connection, and memorability to ideas and concepts.

Some of the world's most successful leaders have been known for their ability to tell stories that effect change. Abraham Lincoln, Walt Disney, Steve Jobs, Sheryl Sandberg, Warren Buffett, and Richard Branson are masters of the art. They created social change, brought families and friends together, built empires, and revolutionized the world by inspiring and engaging those around them through stories.

Even if you don't consider yourself a particularly talented storyteller, storytelling, even in its most elementary form, remains the most effective way to influence others. Stories are affirming, interesting, and emotional. They bring movements to life by driving change in human behavior. Starting with cave paintings and evolving to electronic media, storytelling has been a staple of human development, inspiration, group mentality, and change from the earliest beginnings of culture.

Organizations such as Microsoft, Motorola, Berkshire Hathaway, Saatchi & Saatchi, Procter & Gamble, NASA, and the World Bank have successfully used storytelling to transform their organization and culture.

Kimberly-Clark incorporates storytelling skills into its leadership training and uses innovative approaches like a television-style comedy called the iTent to dramatize learning on topics such as inclusive management.[15]

Nike has a number of senior executives who serve as "corporate storytellers" to ensure people understand and know the company's heritage. They believe that the stories they tell about their past help shape their future.[16]

Stories are a central part of 3M's identity.[17] The organization trains sales representatives to tell stories that paint pictures for customers, showing how their products will help those customers succeed. They also use storytelling for recognition and to celebrate successful programs. The company replaced bulleted lists on strategic planning documents with "strategic narratives" to clarify thinking and capture the excitement and imagination of ideas.

Even traditional PowerPoint platforms are transforming to help presenters tell stories rather than click through lifeless slides. Software applications like Microsoft's Sway, as well as alternatives like Prezi and Canva, are making it easier to add pictures and videos to bring ideas to life through stories.

In Dan Schawbel's *Forbes* article "How to Use Storytelling as a Leadership Tool," he lists the five most common circumstances where stories are used most effectively in business.[18] They are:

- inspiring the organization,
- setting a vision,
- teaching important lessons,
- defining culture and values,
- explaining who you are and what you believe.

All leaders should make an active and intentional effort to look and listen for stories to share that help support and illustrate the outcomes they desire.

Chapter Questions

From a leadership perspective, ask and answer the following questions. Ask others in your business and those you do business with, too. As Pitasky suggests, build a narrative around your responses and the responses you receive. Does this narrative accurately represent your organization and what it wants and needs to be?

- Does my organization embrace servant leadership and a culture of selfless behavior?
- Does my organization measure its worth based on the social and economic value it creates for others, communities, and the world?

- Is my organization making a difference in the lives of others and in the communities it serves?
- Are the leaders in my organization listening to and caring for people?
- Are leaders in my organization sharing stories to reinforce and inspire a winning culture?

Notes

1. "Starbucks Supplier Social Responsibility Standards: Manufactured Goods and Services." *Starbucks*. www.starbucks.com/assets/1deb372ee3d840179e59c5b9c21cd5fe.pdf.
2. "Sourcing." *Starbucks*. www.starbucks.com/responsibility/sourcing.
3. George N. Root III. "The Advantages of the Servant Leadership Style." *Small Business Chron.*
4. Jeb Blount. *People Follow You: The Real Secret to What Matters Most in Leadership.* New York: Wiley, November 15, 2011.
5. "Washington's Best Workplaces Announcement." *Puget Sound Business Journal*, June, 2014. www.bizjournals.com/seattle/blog/2014/06/85-companies-named-washingtons-best-workplaces.html#g23.
6. Charles Riley and Poppy Harlow. "Gravity Payments CEO Defends $70,000 Minimum Salary." *CNN*, August 10, 2015. money.cnn.com/2015/08/09/news/gravity-payments-dan-price-70k-salary/.
7. Chris Isidore. "$70,000 Promise Brings Flood of New Clients and Job Applicants." *CNN*, April 20, 2015. money.cnn.com/2015/04/20/news/companies/pay-raises-new-business/.
8. Tess Townsend. "Dan Price Gave His Employees a Raise: In Return, They Bought Him a Tesla." *Inc.*, July 15, 2016. www.inc.com/tess-townsend/these-employees-thanked-their-boss-with-a-tesla.html.
9. Lead Strategic. leadstrategic.com/2012/10/17/my-favorite-greenleaf-quotes/.
10. Larry C. Spears. "Character and Servant Leadership: Ten Characteristics of Effective, Caring Leaders." *The Spears Center*, 2010. https://www.researchgate.net/publication/252418859_Character_and_Servant-Leadership_Ten_Characteristics_of_Effective_Caring_Leaders.

11. "Altruism." *Psychology Today*. www.psychologytoday.com/basics/altruism.
12. Eric Aronson. "The Chinese Bamboo Tree." January 1, 2009. donmillereducation.com/journal/the-chinese-bamboo-tree/.
13. Noah St. John. "Why I Hate the Bamboo Story." www.earlytorise.com/why-i-hate-the-bamboo-story-2/.
14. Malcolm Gladwell. *Outliers: The Story of Success*. Boston: Little, Brown and Company, October 29, 2008. Pp. 48–50.
15. The Gronstedt Group. "Kimberly Clark: Transforming Culture with Transmedia Storytelling." gronstedtgroup.com/project/kimberly-clark-transforming-culture-with-transmedia-storytelling/.
16. Eric Ransdell. "The Nike Story? Just Tell It!" *Fast Company*, December 31, 1999. www.fastcompany.com/38979/nike-story-just-tell-it.
17. Gordon Shaw, Robert Brown, and Philip Bromiley. "Strategic Stories: How 3M Is Rewriting Business Planning." *Harvard Business Review*, May–June 1998. hbr.org/1998/05/strategic-stories-how-3m-is-rewriting-business-planning.
18. Dan Schawbel. "How to Use Storytelling as a Leadership Tool." *Forbes*, August 13, 2012. www.forbes.com/sites/danschawbel/2012/08/13/how-to-use-storytelling-as-a-leadership-tool/#7b61077a7ac9.

Conclusion

To truly change the world, you must run a great business.

—Louis Efron

Purpose Meets Execution is the organizational culture and mindset—supported by the right leadership, values, actions, and people—that creates profitable and sustainable businesses.

The heart of Purpose Meets Execution is the idea that accelerated engagement of people drives organizational results. Without a culture of high engagement, only limited success is possible. The need for people in your business to understand how their personal purpose connects to the larger organizational purpose is key to this engagement and alignment. Without it, organizations may have an army of nine-to-fivers delivering what needs to be delivered to keep the business temporarily afloat, but they will fall well short of making a meaningful and lasting difference to customers, the community, and humanity.

A closing illustration of what such engagement looks like came to me just days before starting to write my concluding thoughts for this book. It was from Miller Milling, the fourth largest milling business in the United State—supplier of flour to Jimmy John's, Kraft, Walmart, and many other name brands.

The example played out during a remarkable tour of a fully operational and profitable 1896 mill in New Prague, Minnesota. I was touring the mill in preparation for an executive retreat I facilitated.

Cole, a self-proclaimed "milling geek" and head miller, turned what was originally scheduled as a twenty-minute walkthrough into a tour that lasted almost three hours. He showed me every inch of the mill and walked me through the entire milling process, from the unloading of raw grain from trucks to the loading of high-quality bags of flour leaving the facility. It was impressive, and I must admit that my fascination with the history, process, and business were big contributing factors to the length of the tour. However, Cole was more than happy to show me everything. He embodies one of my favorite quotes: "If you love what you do, you never work a day in your life."

When I speak about people working in a business who are fully aligned with their organization's purpose, Cole is the poster person. Both Miller Milling and Cole exist to feed the world high-quality and healthy grain-based products. If you were to meet Cole, his alignment would be more than clear, highlighted by his high level of engagement, passion for what he does, and an educational background in milling. He does not have a job at Miller Milling—he has the life he wants because of his work for the company. Milling is in his blood.

Once people—employees, contractors, vendors, and customers—understand why your organization exists, it is easier for them to execute on actions that are connected to helping you fulfill your organizational purpose. For the people working in your business, connection is every action they take in their jobs, minute by minute, hour by hour, and day by day, and their understanding of how their actions move the organization's bigger picture forward. On the customer side, this connection manifests itself in customers buying your products and promoting them to others. However strong an organization's purpose may be, it is useless without the ability to effectively execute on it.

Cole, again, provided me a fresh example of what executional excellence looks like in practice. He knows how the work he does every day helps fulfill his and Miller Milling's purpose. I witnessed his attention to the people he manages, operational details, product quality, and mill safety, all fueling his every action. The mills' high people engagement, performance, and exemplary quality and safety records reflect this focus.

Cole told me a story about the cleaners who work at his mill. "They keep our equipment running well and our people safe," he says. I did not know it at the time, but airborne particles of grain are highly flammable. In fact, without proper cleaning and dust collection, a flour mill is basically a ticking bomb. The fact that cleaners at Cole's mill realize they are keeping people safe so they can make more flour to feed the world is a grand example of connecting an organization's *why* (its purpose) with its *what* (its mission) to get to its *where* (its vision).

The only way to truly make a significant and positive impact with your organization and possibly change the world, if that is your intention, is to make more money and invest those funds back into your business to hire more like-minded people who drive your purpose forward and expand it. If you are in the health-care industry, helping people live better lives, it only makes sense that you would want to touch as many lives as possible. If you help feed the world, you will want to touch every hungry person on the planet. If you sell safe, affordable automobile tires, you want every driver on a budget to have your product on her car. If you are making it possible for people to afford and enjoy retirement, you want the resources to educate the masses of young people who need to start saving. If your company serves other businesses, you will want the most innovative and comprehensive products and services to support the success of your customers' organizations.

If you are not making the money you need to produce, innovate, and distribute or deliver your products or services, as well as to hire more people to expand your organization's reach, your ability to positively impact the lives of others will be limited.

In a commercial business, profit is a mandatory element to fulfilling an organization's purpose—regardless of the industry or geographical location.

In not-for-profit organizations, the same principle applies to fundraising. In charity work, your product is your cause, and your customers are your donors and contributors. The more you can sell the cause to others, the more money you will bring to your charity, and the more you will be able to fund projects to improve or eradicate the problem.

An organizational purpose is fulfilled only when it is fueled by executional excellence. To make a meaningful and sustainable positive impact on your customers, community, and the world, you must have a clear purpose *and* run a great business.

The next-generation workforce—and in fact, as KPMG discovered, other generations too—are not interested in *work.* They are not lazy. They don't think the world owes them a living. They want more out of life and want to leave the world a better place because they lived. Customers want this, too. If skilled and trained leaders and managers can:

- effectively communicate and align organizational and people purpose,
- focus on executional outcomes that align with organizational purpose,
- sincerely care about the *life* success of people, and
- pull people together through shared purpose,

organizations will accelerate people engagement and drive profits—creating winning, meaningful, and lasting results for humanity.

Acknowledgments

A big thank-you to the following people, who have played a special part in the birth of this book. You are only as good as those around you in life. I consider myself very blessed.

Evie Efron, Anya Rose Efron, Ella Brae Efron, Ben Maller, Brian Mohr, Max Hansen, Peter Winick, David Sturt, Dan Henkle, Waldo Waldman, Jan Rutherford, Bruce Pfau, Mehran Assadi, David Ossip, Scott Pitasky, Mike Brady, Bruce Broussard, Carey Smith, Kevin Cleary, Cher Murphy, Jennifer Knickerbocker, Jeremy Blank, Larry C. Spears, Johnny Earle, Cole Schroeder, Tracy Beyer, Lauren Greathouse, Akash Hira, Jávier Jácome, Deepak Abrol, Anne Isenhower, Jessica Branco, Ashley Gonias, Eric Severson, Mark Christensen, Jill Friedlander, Erika Heilman, and the team at Bibliomotion and Taylor & Francis.

An additional thank-you goes to my remarkable editors, Elena Todorova and Susan Lauzau. Also, thank you to Ann Rhoades for the wonderful foreword and to Joseph Michelli, Melissa Daimler, Lacey Leone McLaughlin, Matthew Fehling, Shawn Murphy, Ryan McCarty, Chester Elton, Cameron Herold, and Dr. Emad Rahim for their thoughtful endorsements.

Thank you, all!

Bibliography

Ariely, Dan. "What Makes Us Feel Good about Our Work?" TED Talk, October 2012. www.ted.com/talks/dan_ariely_what_makes_us_feel_good_about_our_work.

Barsade, Sigal, and Olivia A. O'Neill. "Employees Who Feel Love Perform Better." *Harvard Business Review*, January 13, 2014. https://hbr.org/2014/01/employees-who-feel-love-perform-better.

Blount, Jeb. *People Follow You: The Real Secret to What Matters Most in Leadership*. New York: Wiley, 2011.

Bonanos, Christopher. *Instant: The Story of Polaroid*. New Haven, CT: Princeton Architectural Press, September 26, 2012.

Christensen, Clayton M. *The Innovator's Dilemma* (Management of Innovation and Change). Cambridge, MA: Harvard Business Review, 1997.

Covey, Stephen. *Leading at the Speed of Trust*. http://www.speedoftrust.com/events/Leading-at-the-Speed-of-Trust.

Deloitte. *Culture of Purpose: A Business Imperative*. New York: Deloitte, 2013. https://www2.deloitte.com/us/en/pages/about-deloitte/articles/culture-of-purpose.html.

Gleeson, Brent. "7 Simple Ways to Lead by Example." *Inc. Magazine*, April 23, 2013. http://www.inc.com/brent-gleeson/7-ways-to-lead-by-example.html.

Greenleaf, Robert K., and Larry C. Spears. *Servant Leadership: A Journey into the Nature of Legitimate Power and Greatness 25th Anniversary Edition*. Mahwah, NJ: Paulist Press, 1977.

Niu, David. *Careercation: Trading Briefcase for Suitcase to Find Entrepreneurial Happiness*. Seattle, WA: TINYhr, 2014.

Pink, Daniel. *Drive*. New York: Riverhead Books, 2011.

Sisodia, Rahendra, David B. Wolfe, and Jagdish N. Sheth. *Firms of Endearment*. Upper Saddle River, NJ: Wharton School Publishing, 2007.

Rath, Tom, and Barry Conchie. *Strengths Based Leadership*. New York: Gallup Press, 2013.

Rhoades, Ann. *Built on Values*. New York: Wiley, 2010.

Root, George N., III. "The Advantages of the Servant Leadership Style." *Small Business Chron*. http://smallbusiness.chron.com/advantages-servant-leadership-style-11693.html.

Rutherford, Jan. *The Littlest Green Beret: On Self-Reliant Leadership*. Saxonburg, PA: Pylon Publishing, 2011.

Schawbel, Dan. "How to Use Storytelling as a Leadership Tool." *Forbes*, August 13, 2012. www.forbes.com/sites/danschawbel/2012/08/13/how-to-use-storytelling-as-a-leadership-tool/#7b61077a7ac9.

Sinek, Simon. *Start with Why: How Great Leaders Inspire Everyone to Take Action*. New York: Portfolio, 2011.

Sturt, David. *Great Work: How to Make a Difference People Love*. Burlington, Canada: O.C. Tanner, 2014.

Waldman, Rob. *Never Fly Solo*. New York: McGraw-Hill, 2010.

Index

About the Author

Louis Efron is founder of The Voice of Purpose and Purpose Meets Execution. Author of *How to Find a Job, Career and Life You Love,* he is also a contributing writer for *Forbes* and *Huffington Post*. Efron's career credits include head of global employee engagement for Tesla Motors, international VP of HR for JDA Software, VP of human resources for the Fortune 300 medical device company Stryker, and Broadway theatre.

An award-winning human resources executive, entrepreneur, writer, theatre director, producer, consultant, and speaker, Efron is also founder of the charity World Child Cancer USA. He has lived and worked throughout the United States, Europe, Africa, and Asia. He studied Labor Relations at Cornell University, New York State School of Industrial and Labor Relations, and Advanced Leadership at Harvard Business School. He holds a BA from California State University, Fullerton, as well as a BS and JD from Saratoga University School of Law. He and his wife are proud parents of two beautiful daughters.

Visit Louis at PurposeMeetsExecution.com.